A WORD FOR ALL SEASONS

SERMONS FROM HENRY MITCHELL

HENRY H. MITCHELL

FOREWORD BY
AIDSAND F. WRIGHT-RIGGINS III

JUDSON PRESS
PUBLISHERS SINCE 1824

Join our mailing list for updates and special offers.
www.judsonpress.com/mailing_list.cfm

A Word for All Seasons: Sermons from Henry Mitchell

Judson Press has made every effort to trace the ownership of all quotes. In the event of a question arising from the use of a quote, we regret any error made and will be pleased to make the necessary correction in future printings and editions of this book.

Bible quotations in this volume are from *The Holy Bible*, King James Version.

Interior design by Crystal Devine.

Cover design by Tobias Becker and Bird Box Design.

Library of Congress Cataloging-in-Publication Data

Mitchell, Henry H., 1919-
    A word for all seasons : sermons from Henry Mitchell / Henry H. Mitchell ; foreword by Aidsand F. Wright-Riggins. -- 1st ed.
        p. cm.
    ISBN 978-0-8170-1722-4 (pbk. : alk. paper) 1. Sermons, American-- African American authors. 2. Occasional sermons. I. Title.
    BV4253.M536 2012
    252'.061--dc23
                                2012018093

Printed in the U.S.A.

First Edition, 2012.

CONTENTS

FOREWORD

I'VE BEEN AN ORDAINED minister for almost forty years. My pulpit ministry has been roughly divided in two seasons: for the first two decades, preaching every Sunday as the pastor of local congregations and for the last twenty years, preaching two or three times each month in my role as a denominational leader. By far, the most challenging preaching assignments for me have been answering the call to preach on "Special Days." Just recently while playing a round of golf with three of my pastor friends, each one in turn asked me to preach at a "special day" service at his church. All three agreed that, having preached so many Mother's Day, Usher's Day, or Stewardship Sunday messages, they had very little left to say.

Whether one has been at this task for four years or forty, when it comes to special days, the preacher will inevitably ask, "What then shall I preach?" *A Word for All Seasons: Sermons from Henry Mitchell* is written to help servants of the Word to wrestle effectively with that question. I think of this volume as a "sermon starter," kindling one's imagination as the preacher ponders a fresh word for the coming special day.

Moreover, *A Word for All Seasons* goes beyond the question of "What shall I preach?" Henry H. Mitchell provides proven and practical guidance to help answer the question, "*How* shall I preach?" as well. I am quite certain that the main reason I was the recipient of a Most Outstanding Preacher award when I graduated from seminary years ago was because, as the only African American in my seminary class, I was granted a special dispensation to study with Henry Mitchell, who had just completed his first book, *Black Preaching*. While my classmates were studying homiletics as an exercise that was almost totally cerebral and cognitive in its development and aim, I was blessed to learn the sacred art under the tutelage of Dr. Mitchell, then Dean of the Ecumenical Center for Black Church Studies in Los Angeles, California.

What I came to understand from Dr. Mitchell was that all good preaching—black, white, or otherwise—is a "meeting," or what he described as an experiential encounter. The gospel message engages both head and heart and has a volitional purpose. Professor Mitchell hammered it home to me, and to the thousands of preachers he has taught since, that the beginning point of a powerful message is not "What are you trying to say?" but "What are you aiming to move the hearer to do?"

No surprise, then, that in these pages readers will find help for remixing Sunday messages that traditionally focus on an occasion—Youth Day, Labor Day, Men's Day, etc.—into an experience that enables a transformative personal and communal encounter. Readers will discover tools such as storytelling, imagination, and speaking in the vernacular of one's hearers, all of which contribute to more effective preaching. They will also learn about the "Moves" of a sermon that usher a congregation from being hearers only to doers also of the Word.

Henry H. Mitchell is not one of those homiletics professors who has a lofty résumé but no practical skill as a preacher. Now in his nineties, Mitchell is still regularly invited to grace the pulpit of some of our nation's most noted churches—and not only on special days! As my grandmother would say, "Henry Mitchell can surely tell it!"

I am proud that I am one of many hundreds of men and women who claim Henry H. Mitchell as a father in the ministry.

Rev. Dr. Aidsand F. Wright-Riggins III
Executive Director, American Baptist Home Mission Societies
Chief Executive Officer, Judson Press

PREFACE

THE PREACHER/PASTOR is confronted constantly with the challenge of delivering messages for special occasions that are interesting, relevant, and fully based on biblical authority. The occasions range from annual days on the church calendar to celebrations of secular holidays. Congregational politics demand a pulpit relating once per year to the young people, the pastor's anniversary, or stewardship, to mention just a few. Faithful pastors and lay leaders offer their level-best prayer discipline and work habits to the God who called them. They are meeting the challenge. Indeed, it does happen, from time to time, that such leaders and preaching are blessed with a harvest of saved and changed souls in Christ.

After more than seventy years of preaching and of teaching, I dare to pick out of "my barrel" a few samples of fresh, biblical approaches to offer here. I do so in the hope that they will be used of God to encourage and stir up the gifts and growth of local pastors, seminarians, lay leaders, and students of the Bible.

This is also a kind of personal homiletic heritage for me. It is written with great gratitude to all whom God graciously sent to help me grow—from the time that I was licensed to preach in January of 1939 until now. While nearly all of my mentors are gone, I pray this sharing may help their heirs, as their forebears so marvelously blessed me.

INTRODUCTION

ONE HARDLY EXPECTS much of an introduction for a book of sermons; they tend to be self-explanatory. This volume, however, has a few features not often, if ever, found in collections of gospel messages. These resources are offered to facilitate the choice of sermon texts and themes for special days and occasions. The assumption has been that it is not enough just to bless the honorees with biblical mention of their roles in the kingdom of God. They are worthy of more than a kindly pat on the back.

Furthermore, the need for freshness and depth is at least as great on special days as on ordinary Sundays. In an effort to leave the beaten path and enhance interest, I have offered here titles like "Jesus Christ, Investment Counselor," for such a time as Stewardship Sunday. The goal is fresh insight rather than cleverness for the sake of cleverness.

I have the profound conviction that while the gospel is expressed in ideas, it fulfills its purpose in experiential encounter. We need to make sense, but ultimately we design an experience of the gospel that makes the idea or doctrine come alive. This is not to be seen as recent theory, however. Jesus used metaphors and narratives, which we call parables. Jesus did not challenge us with an abstract idea like "Be ye compassionate!"; he used a narrative about a Good Samaritan. When one is aware that the Scripture calls for narration, one can follow the rules that make for good, focused gospel storytelling. Thus, each sermon is introduced by its behavioral purpose, drawn from and implied by the sermon texts, to facilitate focus. (This rule is enlarged in *Celebration and Experience in Preaching*.)[1]

The behavioral purpose is counterpart to the traditional theme; it is the concrete action that causes the abstract theme, such as Women's Day or Youth Sunday, to come alive in a transformative way. Here again, Jesus is the model. The vicarious experience that goes with hearing the story changes the hearer by the power of the Holy Spirit, using identification with the main character of the parable.

It is my hope, of course, that the messages in this volume will be seen to exemplify these insights into sermon structure and that the reader/preacher will develop skills parallel to the examples. Any text noted here may be used to preach a timeless gospel at any spot on the calendar.

Note
1. Abingdon Press, Revised edition, September 2008.

1

MOTHER'S DAY

THE CELEBRATION OF Mother's Day is relatively recent, but most people—races, classes, ages, or communities—take few if any days more seriously. Like other major holidays, Mother's Day has become a much-commercialized holiday. Many people want to show appreciation, and other people capitalize on the uncertainty as to how to celebrate motherhood appropriately. All too many mothers are praised to the heights and deluged with flowers, candy, and bling-bling, only to be nailed back into the same restricted role in which tradition has held them since prehistoric times.

The women who have broken out of this mold are often thought to be hardly worthy of trust, especially if they seem proud about evading motherhood and domestic chores. If modern family economics requires two incomes, those chores require division as well. Seldom, however, are they divided equally, if at all. Yet many males wax tearful about their mothers in the old mold, all the while hoping to find a blessing of the same from their own wives. The exploitation noted here is deeply imbedded in the culture and extremely difficult to dislodge. Such advantages will not yield to direct attack or countercultural confrontation, so long as male dominance keeps its preference among so many, male and female.

Head-to-head confrontation against established culture is futile. Folk mores have lived too long and have served too well to discard now. An indirect tactic at a much deeper level is preferable to a shallow challenge. For instance, no amount of Mother's Day gifts and ritual can compensate for exploitation, no matter how disguised. Actually, there can be no true love of a mother whom one exploits and does not deeply respect. Aretha Franklin's song about asking for respect would probably be a preferable comment.

With this view of women, and avoiding confrontations, the behavioral purpose of the following sermon is to move male hearers to profound respect and awesome admiration for the mothers in their lives. This is achieved by a new vision of a wonderful woman overlooked: Jochebed, the magnificent mother of Moses. After fitting recognition of mothers, this sensitive respect is accomplished through the following moves in consciousness:

Move 1: Jochebed's plan to save her son was brilliant, and her trust in God was powerful, as are many mothers' today.

Move 2: Jochebed taught God-given ethnic and spiritual self-esteem extremely well, and so do many mothers today.

Move 3: We celebrate Jochebed, mother of Moses, and Mary, mother of Jesus, and their huge and blessed influence of our history and the world's.

SERMON TEXT: NUMBERS 26:59
And the name of Amram's wife was Jochebed, the daughter of Levi, whom her mother bare to Levi in Egypt: and she bare unto Amram Aaron and Moses, and Miriam their sister.

SERMON SUPPLEMENTARY TEXT: EXODUS 2:1-10
And there went a man of the house of Levi, and took to wife a daughter of Levi. And the woman conceived, and bare a son: and when she saw him that he was a goodly child, she hid him three months. And when she could no longer hide him, she took for him an ark of bulrushes, and daubed it with slime and with pitch, and put the child therein; and she laid it in the flags by the river's brink. And his sister stood afar off, to wit what would be done to him. And the daughter of Pharaoh came down to wash herself at the river; and her maidens walked along by the river's side; and when she saw the ark among the flags, she sent her maid to fetch it. And when she had opened it, she saw the child: and, behold, the babe wept. And she had compassion on him, and said, This is one of the Hebrews' children. Then said his sister to Pharaoh's daughter, Shall I go and call to thee a nurse of the Hebrew women, that she may nurse the child for thee? And Pharaoh's daughter said to her, Go. And the maid went and called the child's mother. And Pharaoh's daughter said unto her, Take this child away, and nurse it for me, and I will give thee thy wages. And the woman took the child, and nursed it. And the child grew, and she brought him unto Pharaoh's daughter, and he became her son. And she called his name Moses: and she said, Because I drew him out of the water.

Moses' Mother: Model for Modern Moms

I invite you this Mother's Day morning to go with me, in your mind's eye, to the maximum-security prison where I found the Bible verse for our text. I had arrived early at Folsom

Prison, near Sacramento, to speak at an Emancipation Day celebration. Their magnificent male chorus was still rehearsing when I took a seat in a small room at the side of the auditorium to listen.

A prisoner in an off-white uniform attracted my attention and struck up a conversation. Or rather, I should have called it an examination. Learning that I was a preacher, he bombarded me with questions from the Bible. In many cases, he knew the answer, and I didn't. I was most embarrassed when I did not even know the name of Moses' mother. Only three years earlier I had finished classes at Union Theological Seminary, what was thought to be the finest Protestant seminary in the world, and I didn't even know Moses' momma's name! I could recite a whole chapter with ease, but I did not have a clue about her name. I now realize how and why; this did not just happen. Let's look briefly at that, and then listen to her powerful story, pondering what it means for us today.

The Bible itself hardly knows her name. The men who recalled the story of Moses' birth (Exodus 2:1-10) tell who Moses' mother's father was but do not mention her name at all. Numbers 26:59 tells us her name was Jochebed, and then names Levi, her father, and Amram, her husband, period—not another word about her. Bible policy seems to have intended to omit mothers' names from genealogies, except in the first chapter of Matthew, which leads up to Jesus. Otherwise, important women, like Joanna, a leading lady supporter of Jesus, and Huldah, the woman whose approval of Bible manuscripts was needed, were defined by their husbands and not by who they were in their own right. It is only right that we ignore this unjust tradition and give Jochebed full credit by name in the following fascinating sermon story.

After Joseph died in Egypt, pharaohs who did not know Joseph enslaved the children of Israel. Nevertheless, even in slavery they prospered and multiplied so rapidly that the Egyptians feared they would be overpowered. Egypt was scared, like South Carolina when its population was 75 percent slave in the early years. The more the cruel taskmasters crushed and oppressed the Israelites, the more they increased. The king ordered the Hebrew midwives to kill all the male infants, but of course the midwives made clever excuses and disobeyed Pharaoh in order to obey God.

Into this hostile climate was born a fine son to the union of Amram and Jochebed. No way was she going to let the king take this fine child's life. She hid him for three months, but then he got too big and healthy to hide. With no recorded help from Amram, she devised an ark of woven bulrushes and made it watertight with pitch. She set it afloat with baby Moses in it among the marsh flowers by the river, so it wouldn't drift away. She also carefully taught her daughter, Miriam, what to do. Miriam was maybe nine or ten years old. She was to skip about and play on top of a mound close by, always keeping an eye on her little brother. It was a lot of responsibility for a child that young, but Miriam was delighted she was so dependable. And, let me tell you, that little girl gave an Academy Award-worthy performance!

When Pharaoh's daughter came to bathe in the river, her attendants spotted the baby and brought him to her royal highness. As God so often equips babies to do, the child stole her heart immediately, even though she was almost certain he was a Hebrew, a slave supposed to be dead. Meanwhile, Miriam played nosy child and edged her way into the onlookers. When it was clear that they planned to keep the child, Miriam childishly piped up, "Ma'am, I happen to know a wet nurse you could probably get to take care of him 'til he can walk and talk and fit in at the palace. Want me to see if I can get her to come?" The princess said, "Do that, but be quick about it."

Jochebed had hidden close by; to be sure there were no accidents. Therefore, Miriam brought her to the princess almost instantly. Her highness hired Jochebed on the spot to nurse her own baby. It was about as slick and clever as it could get. Everything stayed on schedule until Moses had moved to the palace, finished school, and was able to go about on his own as a young man. It is a fascinating story, but it is far more than a tale to tell. Jochebed's part is loaded with meaning, especially this Mother's Day.

The first thing young Jochebed says to me is this: "My body may be in chains, but my soul is free to trust my righteous and provident Gawd all the way. Pharaoh's gov'ment may have the authority to kill my son, but my Gawd gave me some wits and cunning, with the powers to go against Pharaoh. I knowed it was dan'gous, but Gawd wanted me to be as clever as I could, and the Lord Gawd did all the rest that was needed." The noble attitude and courageous idea in this imaginary speech is familiar to all of us who have known and lived among ex-slaves in our own early years.

I never saw my father's father's mother, but I am sure my dear great-grandmother would have said much the same thing. She was clever and tough and trusting enough to take (sneak) the Underground Railroad from Southampton County, on the lower tier of Virginia, all the way across Virginia, Pennsylvania, and western New York to London, Ontario, Canada. I take it personally, because my Grandpa Mitchell's mother had him born free. Nevertheless, I am just as proud of my Grandpa Estis, born a slave on the west end of the same lower tier of Virginia, near a village called Kenbridge. I just wish every African American child could know how faithful, courageous, and free in spirit his own great-grandparents were. What an example!

The second thing Jochebed says as I meditate is, "You don't know what kind of talent Gawd done give you or your chil'uns 'til you try it out. Iffen Gawd say do it, don't worry 'bout how hard it is, 'cause Gawd knowed what gifts he done give you 'fore he tol' you what to do. No slave in the hand of Gawd is stripped of the power to do things. As long as Gawd is just, and all power is in his hands, we'uns can do a heap of things the world tried to tell us we couldn't."

Imagine poor Miriam, nine or ten years old, with the very life of her baby brother in her little-girl hands! Imagine all the things that could go wrong, and all she has to defend herself are her mind and her mouth. Her faith is there in the sense that she caught it from Momma, but she hasn't been praying like adults. She only knows what Momma prayed and what Momma said to do. The acting role Momma gave her is something she has been playing at ever since she was five. She plunges into an awesome responsibility with an admirable working confidence.

What Jochebed did for Miriam's self-confidence is exactly what more mothers today need to do for our children. Hard times made many of us what we are, and we make a mistake when we try to shield our children from some of the challenges of hard necessity. The Great Depression of the 1930s was part of the fundamental training that got many of us through, and what we called Mother Needmore was the chief instructor. And Mother Needmore is back with us.

My mom was another Jochebed. She had no questions like, "Do you think you can do it?" Whatever it was, the sweetly spoken word was, "Please fix it." I was maybe twelve when "it" was a washing machine sounding like it was cracking up. My thought was that if she was willing to risk it, I was glad to act like a mechanic until I could see what was going on. I knit my brow and cleaned all that never-changed dirty grease out of the box of gears that rocked the cylinder full of dirty clothes. Anybody could then see where the gear teeth were missing. I biked to a store and bought replacement parts, refilled the lubricant, cut out a cork gasket, and bolted the gearbox cover. To my great delight, it worked. I shall never cease to praise God for a mother who protected me from dangers when needed but who sent me with confidence through the bulrushes of life and prayed for me until I got all the way through, by the grace of God.

A third thing I heard from Jochebed in that meditation was something like, "We told that child all about our people, and how we was proud of them and their religion. Whilst we had him in our house, he learned all the Hebrew children's chants and prayers and dances. We tol' him 'bout slavery and what to tell masters an' what not to say. I was glad he was going to have all the good stuff of the son of a princess and grandson of the pharaoh. But he musn't ever forget who he was, and to come and see about us ev'ry now and then."

Lessons like self-esteem are caught from experience, and that mother-guided experience in the slave quarter yielded powerful identification and loyalty in Moses, so much so that he killed two Egyptians whom he saw abusing his people. While he had to flee Pharaoh's justice, the years in Midian were not wasted. They served to prepare Moses spiritually for his return and the leading of his Hebrew kinfolk out of slavery in Egypt and on to the Promised Land.

Jochebed exemplifies a mother's pride in her God-given ethnic identity, her healthy racial self-esteem, as well as her faith. The two were inseparable. Out of her formative influence on young Moses grew the Moses-led exodus and the fresh revelation of our omnipotent God as faithful, just, and righteous. Egypt was a social context fraught with constant efforts to keep slaves down and to exploit them. To the contrary, Jochebed transmitted her contagious faith to her son Moses. No doubt she used the same methods that he later advised in Deuteronomy 6:7 for the training of children under oppression and tempted to copy their captors' attractive culture: "And you shall teach God's commandments diligently to your children. You shall casually talk about them when you're sitting at home, and when you're walking down the street, when you're going to bed, and when you are getting up" (author's paraphrase). How else could Moses have so successfully resisted the option of Egyptian princedom?

No amount of royal privilege and unjust advantage could entice him to identify with the palace position and disown his true self. Due in part to Jochebed, Moses and the rest of us have learned how to keep from being swept away in the worldly majority.

My mother, in Jochebed's footsteps, also bore the burden of the crusade for self-esteem, freedom, and justice in her time. I can't forget her declaring the injustice of the city gerrymandering of African American children out of our elementary school district in 1930. During World War I, we had increased considerably in an area adjacent to white privilege. The pharaoh class wanted us out and drew some strangely crooked boundaries to achieve segregation in Ohio. In protest, my sweet Christian mother tongue-lashed the white principal with facts. (She later proceeded to organize.) At something like nine, ten, and eleven, her three sons witnessed the encounter with arrogant joy, as the principal turned bright red. Little wonder that all three of her sons and, later, her daughter grew up to be civil rights activists, all under the influence of a modern Jochebed and in a Christian mode. There are many more women of faith and courage whose witness deserves sincere appreciation, too.

The need for more women like Jochebed continues, however. In the meantime, we must never forget to keep on thanking the first one, the one we overlooked for so long. An astounding proportion of our Hebrew-Christian tradition worldwide and that of quite a few millions of Muslims besides all trace directly or indirectly back to Moses' influence and his deliverance of his people—all of this under the influence of the faith and courageous ingenuity of Momma Jochebed. But that is only the start of it all. It is quite literally true that the hand that rocks the cradle rules.

The first book of the Old Testament to be put into formal writing was Exodus, and much, if not all of it, is attributed to Moses. Virtually all of Old Testament tradition focuses on the law of Moses. This means that even such a document as the United States Constitution is in the tradition of detailed legal and moral codification launched by Moses when there was nothing this committed to impartial justice, and nothing done this comprehensively.

The very idea of one God rather than a god among many gods owes much to Moses and to the first law of the Decalogue. Thus, again, do we have to look to Jochebed, Moses' first teacher. And the idea that such a one God is unchangeably righteous is likewise debtor to Moses and to the woman who raised him and who was used by God to help order his concepts of justice and of right and wrong. The worship of Baal, with all its alcoholic and sexual orgies, is still abroad in the earth by other names. Can you fancy a world without the moral influence and stable justice of Moses and Momma Jochebed?

I shudder to think of a world without Moses. You can think the same of a world without Momma Jochebed. Moreover, something of the same sort can be said of many another mother, with even less printed and spoken credit than Jochebed. The church and civil government and homes especially need to celebrate Jochebed and encourage mothers like her.

Praise God for our mothers, grandmothers, and great-grandmothers, who fought discrimination in schools and jobs and housing to gain what privileges we enjoy today!

Hooray for Jochebed, the mother with love, smarts, and courageous faith enough to save Moses, the father of truly civilized society, moral law, and equal justice!

Praise God for Mary, the mother who with her husband, Joseph, outwitted King Herod to protect her son Jesus, until he could die for the salvation of the whole world!

Hallelujah! Amen!

2

Memorial Day

THIS SERMON'S behavioral purpose is the lessening and ultimate elimination of emotional depression, which is an illness as well as a feeling, a lower emotion only in its earlier stages. Depression includes no joy in life and encourages suicide in the purest or most extreme form of "nothing to live for." Thus this sermon is not a message for Memorial Day weekend only. It may apply to any time of sorrow, occurring at any given point on the church's worship calendar.

When the purpose is so deeply emotional, there is a particular need for care in choosing a fitting genre or experiential encounter with the Word. This sermon has complex structure, but, as a whole, its structure checks out as a classic case study/personality sketch. The third Move points out Elijah's mistakes, and the fourth Move celebrates the apostle Paul's prescription for the case: an expository treatment of the main text. It has two moves of its own, drawn from the main text. The prayer for Elijah's own death in the supplementary text sets the whole sermon as a case study, and provides the behavioral purpose/problem. It could not serve, however, as the main text, because the behavioral purpose and the text have to be positively celebrated in the closing move. Elijah's prayer, "Now take away my life," only impersonates the problem, surely not the behavioral goal. The Moves, then, fall out thus:

Move 1:   Elijah is highly regarded for speaking truth to power, and is careful about his safety.

Move 2:   Elijah wins a power test against 400 false prophets, and supervises their execution.

Move 3:   Elijah flees for his safety, but makes many mistakes, and prays for God to take his life.

Move 4:   We celebrate the main text: the apostle Paul's faith-cure for depression.

A word of warning may be wise for ministry to the greatly depressed. I only wish I could have heard it myself. I did not know how much I needed it. An unwise choice of illustrations can stir up tragic identifications or call up ties too close to other tragic cases. I shudder to think of the damage I could have done before I learned to illustrate from the Bible rather than from the pastor's ministries to depression. For example, teenage traffic deaths are horribly common, and I used one, only to discover that, unbeknown to me, we had had one in the local congregation less than forty-eight hours before preaching time. The seventeen-year-old was lost, taking risks in his new car. He was the only grandson of a deeply attached grandfather who was in the congregation that morning. The grandfather greeted me with gratitude after the service. He could have resented the mere mention of a loss so similar to his. But he was most gracious, and I surely thanked him for thanking me. It would have been better if I had done what I am doing here now: I am diagnosing a distant figure about whom I can be completely candid. Identifying with Elijah, I can set up a less threatening healing encounter for the hearer.

SERMON TEXT: 1 CORINTHIANS 10:13
There hath no temptation taken you but such as is common to man: but God is faithful, who will not suffer you to be tempted above that ye are able; but

will with the temptation also make a way to escape, that ye may be able to bear it.

SERMON SUPPLEMENTARY TEXT: 1 KINGS 19:4
. . . and he requested for himself that he might die, and said, It is enough; now, O LORD, take away my life, for I am not better than my fathers.

How Much You Can Bear?

If someone were to ask you, "What is the worst of the diseases abroad among the citizens of this country?" what would you say? Cancer? Heart trouble? High blood pressure? Diabetes? Well, I would say still another: depression. Why? Because it undermines and intensifies all the others. What do I mean by depression, and how does it differ from grief? A depressed person has no joy, no hope, and no real reason to stay alive on the planet. A grieving person is more likely to focus on the loss of one's beloved, a job, or a home. Grief is limited in time as well as topic, but depression pervades all of life. It knows no boundaries. It infects all ages from the teens to the centenarians, although super seniors are the least likely to yield to senior suicide. The load of grief is shared with companionship and emotional support: it accepts the need for help.

By our definition, Elijah's prayer is a prayer of depression: "O LORD, now take away my life" (1 Kings 19:4). It assumes there is nothing left worth living for. It takes the story behind this pitiful prayer to explain how a prophet of the high standing of Elijah could have hit bottom so hard. It was not always so. Up until he received a threat of death by contract from Queen Jezebel, Elijah had been quite content. He did stay out of the sight of King Ahab, but he was nothing like suicidal. God had fed him well in the wilderness when others were still hungry. And God helped Elijah to show off by accepting his soaking-wet sacrifice by fire. That was a very special favor.

The problem arose because Elijah's victory in the test of the gods of Ahab's prophets gave Elijah authority to order that the four hundred losing prophets be put to death. The record reads as though Elijah must have put some of them to death himself. That really angered Jezebel (1 Kings 19:2); those priests were her private pastors. She ordered Elijah dead within twenty-four hours, and, in her fierce pride, she sent Elijah formal notice. Elijah was scared to death. He called his servant, and they took off for distant Beersheba immediately. It was a wise move, of course.

Elijah walked all the way to Beersheba and left his servant there. Then he walked another whole day into the wilderness, in hiding from Jezebel's hired killers. In this solitude, Elijah prayed right away for God to take him. Then he kept on going for forty more days, and God sent him his daily dinner. He communed with God, but his main word was about how he was the only believer left. God, of course, put a stop to his notion that he was alone, and made him get up and go back to his calling. Thus ends the story that leads up to the desire to die.

I can hear you saying in silence, "That doesn't explain how a great prophet hit bottom." So let me point out Elijah's mistakes that led to that strange desire to die. His first mistake is clear—he gave in to fear. He panicked and ran for his life (1 Kings 19:3). Not that he should not have disappeared, but he lost his most mature wisdom when he yielded to a panic attack.

The second mistake is closely related—he forgot to trust God. In so doing, he also forgot all the ways God had already taken care of him. Fresh in his memory should have been the way God had backed him up in the contest with the priests. God had come to his aid too many times for Elijah to fear that God would desert him now.

Elijah's third mistake was his self-pity. Spiritually and mentally, it is dangerous poison to engage in self-pity. It is the height of self-centeredness to feel sorry for oneself. When trapped in a state of self-pity, one can justify almost anything as self-defense. Further, Jesus plainly stated that whoever seeks to save self shall lose it (Mark 8:35). Highly trained clinical psychologists say the same. We were not made by God to be consumed with pity for self.

The fourth mistake was Elijah's notion that "I only am left, and they're trying to kill me" (1 Kings 19:10,14, author's paraphrase). Like many folks, we consider our problems unique. "You just don't know what I've been through" is a common cry. We deserve special attention, because nobody else has ever had it this hard. This is a special form of self-pity, and it always fails to give the special status we seek.

Elijah's fifth and final mistake is stated in three words: "It is enough." It was parallel to the common ultimatum by which we try to seize control: "I've had all I can take. I can't bear any more." It is a veiled threat, as if to pray, "Almighty God, if you don't rescue me right away, I'll snap and go crazy and embarrass you and all these believers." Such threats are based on the foolish assumption that I know just how much I can stand, and no more. They had not heard many a believer to testify that "in a dire crisis, God blessed me with strength I didn't dream of having. Like two days without a wink of sleep while I cared for my sick child." Nobody really knows her or his limits; only the God who made us knows that. And we don't really need to know. What we need is the faith outlined in the main text. That is the verse in 1 Corinthians 10:13, to which we may already have our Bible open. Let us read it aloud: "There hath no temptation taken you but such as is common to man: but God is faithful, who will not suffer you to be tempted above that ye are able; but will with the temptation also make a way to escape, that ye may be able to bear it."

Our main text starts with Elijah's fourth mistake, the issue of the presumed uniqueness of our troubles, so we move from Elijah's mistakes to Paul's curative response: "There has no problem befallen you that isn't well known among humankind" (1 Corinthians 10:13, author's paraphrase). In other words, many people have faced this before and have come through with flying colors. You needn't think your trouble is unmatched or that you deserve special attention or treatment for an overestimated burden.

This note on survival comes from the same apostle Paul who had learned to be content in whatsoever state he was in (Philippians 4:11). He found serious reason to give thanks in, if not for, everything. It was truth when, in handcuffs and leg irons, he considered himself fortunate that he was privileged to speak in his own defense in King Agrippa's court (Acts 26:2).

To claim to have unique problems is to forget that many have been delivered from troubles as great as or even greater than our own. And, that it was God who made it happen. Paul says that the God who delivered these persons is faithful and trustworthy (1 Corinthians 10:13). God will keep our tests and trials within our abilities to cope. However, if a test does exceed our capacities, God will make a way of escape. Underneath all of this is the belief in the omniscience of God.

This all-knowing attribute is applied to unusual purposes. Omniscience is associated most often with knowledge of scientific data or human history: God the awesome computer intellect who knows everything in all those books in the library. In our context, God's knowledge is seen as a deep sensitivity to human emotional and spiritual need, and we are glad about it on this very personal basis.

It is fascinating how widely this belief in the omniscience of God is embraced in African American culture. It was surely not learned from the teachings of cruel slaveholders. For instance, this exact divine attribute is in an Ashanti praise name for God: *Brekyirihunuade*, which means "he who sees all before and behind."[1] The praise name is interpreted to include what we can bear and much more. This divine wisdom is essential to the application of the all-powerful attribute so pervasive in African traditional religions. Unlimited power without divine wisdom to apply it would be useless or, worse, dangerous. And tests and trials without this guarantee of limits would be hard to endure, especially in the days of slavery. A spiritual sings supportive insight to the limitation of trials, when proclaiming joy that "trouble don't last always."

This certitude of limited trials is sacred theology, but it is in secular folk culture as well. The two are indivisible in African culture. This suggests all the more that this beautiful affirmation came across from Africa and survived despite oppression and suppression. Because this faith was so supportive of survival, it was alive and well prior to the embrace of Christianity and continues to exist in the street until now.

Thus Lola Falana, a star African American singer in poor health, expressed her secular certainty: "God will know what my needs are and will supply. He gives you no more than you can carry."[2] She sought divine help in fulfilling her Las Vegas contract and believed she received it.

A drug lord, indicted for the first time, confidently declared to his fellow inmates in a New Orleans prison holding cell, "God has never put a thing on this earth that he didn't make man strong enough to withstand."[3]

These impressive affirmations are made with no claims of roots in Sunday school or from seats at Grandma's dinner table. They represent authentic folk faith that is alive on its own face value, heard and accepted without suspicion of insincerity or pretense. It is time-tested and required to prove nothing. It is authentic folk wisdom, unencumbered by any missionary claims for credit. It may not be accepted by formal religion as adequate for salvation, but if so, no Christian dare deny that such believers are surely not far from the kingdom.

Meanwhile, another stream of culture was evolving in the black churches, many of them in storefronts in urban areas and all of them affected by what became known as the Great Depression. The blues of the 1920s and later were baptized back into the mother church by a saddened blues musician named Thomas Dorsey. His songs caught on swiftly. They had roots in the culture and were not dependent on the slow processes of folk culture. The songs were promoted by commercialization. The composers printed and sold sheet music all across the United States. Although at first resisted by some as too close to its blues roots, the spread of gospel music was phenomenal. By the end of World War II, gospel songs were part of the standards in the vast majority of black churches. They all had a gospel choir.

Almost as popular as Dorsey's "Precious Lord, Take My Hand" was a gospel song that set our main Bible text to music. It focused on "He knows, yes, he knows, just how much we can bear." Throughout the depths of the Depression and all during World War II, this song continued to spread. In this country still accursed with racial prejudice, segregation, and legalized injustice, this helpful, healing word was sung. It was sung during worship and quietly hummed on the street corner. The apostle Paul's classic word to the Corinthians was included along with pop tunes and in personal repertoires, and it was sung among street people as well as church folk. I know, because I was one.

As a student of culture, I rejoice in this marvelous folk movement of the gospel, in streets as well as churches, but there is another, more important phase. When anybody wants to know how you get a gut-level trust in the Lord who knows how much you can bear, I say, "Open your heart," and it will help a lot if the song you sing and hum all day long is Roberta Martin's gospel song instead of a pop song. Sing it in the morning when you rise, and it will bubble up all day long. By the power of the Holy Spirit, you will sing it right into your very soul.

Notes

1. N. C. Lewter and H. H. Mitchell, *Soul Theology* (Nashville: Abingdon, 1991), 56.
2. Lewter and Mitchell, 1-2.
3. Lewter and Mitchell, 1-2.

3

CHURCH ANNIVERSARY

DURING THE CLOSING years of World War II and the following fourteen years, it was my privilege to work in church extension: launching new congregations for the huge influx of war workers. While the majority came from the rural and semi-rural South, they had no intentions of returning. Supposedly temporary worship spaces in northern California needed to become permanent; nonprofit corporations needed to be established; and buildings needed building or adaptation. All of this meant that in places where the embryo church managed to survive, there would be an anniversary to celebrate every twelve months. Having been the midwife at these births, I preached innumerable anniversary sermons.

For young churches like these, anniversaries have less sense of proud tradition and more of joy just to have survived the innumerable hazards of infant congregations. Memories of divine deliverance keep alive the joy of pioneering. Unforgettable battle scars also remain from the attempts to merge so many different patterns of practice from so many different places. A consensus culture takes years to form, aided by the healing influence of celebrations of individual contributions through the years.

Well-established congregations are likely to have much history and plenty of worship resources, so the tone of the sermon that follows veers toward the needs of the new church. However, the hazards of urban population cycles and social change cause many older churches to share more and more of the challenges faced by the young. The outline of the sermon that follows came from notes for a new church anniversary in the East, while virtually all the illustrations draw from histories of new churches in the West. In the interest of maintaining professional confidence, the names and locations are fictitious.

While the church's founders and first leaders are truly worthy of anniversary honor, the primary behavioral purpose of the sermon is to use that praise to encourage and inspire pastor and congregation to still greater ministries amidst greater, rapid-changing needs. The moves (points become lively encounters) are filled with praiseworthy and moving examples of fruitful ministries now and in the future. These moves provide experiential flow and structure:

Move 1:   We older churches of today are inspired by the great stones on which we were built, and the roots out of which we grew, in Africa and Europe, and then the USA.

Move 2:   We do well to celebrate and emulate specific trials and victories in our own history.

Move 3:   Celebrate the worldwide Christian Church; nothing has prevailed against her.

SERMON TEXT: PSALM 127:1
Except the Lord build the house, they labour in vain that build it: except the Lord keep the city, the watchman waketh but in vain.

SERMON SUPPLEMENTARY TEXT: MATTHEW 16:18
Upon this rock I will build my church; and the gates of hell shall not prevail against it.

Gye Nyame: Unless God

Congratulations on your twentieth birthday as a congregation—a family fellowship of faith—a church of the living God. We have great reason to rejoice, and I am delighted to be invited to your birthday party. Nevertheless, this is a lot more than just a time to sing "Happy Birthday to Ya!" Yes, sing the birthday song, but then it is also time to meditate on how we managed to get here in the first place, and why. Then, before we say, "Goodbye!" it is time to scan the future for a vision as to where ministry goes from here. Our main text for today is Psalm 127:1 [read two times]: "Except the LORD build the house, they labour in vain that build it: except the LORD keep the city, the watchman waketh but in vain."

On our personal birthdays, we tend to take for granted how we got here in the first place. We never reach back and celebrate the miracles of painful birth canals or the marvelous menus God made for babies. Our parties concentrate on children, and parents after the children can walk, talk, think, and work. The only time we thank God for such essentials as food for survival is when we say the grace at the dinner table. For this church's birthday party, I feel guided to lead in the celebration of all the many blessings God has given us, from the first planning and worship on through every one of the following twenty years, lest we forget.

As already announced, our Scripture text is the first verse of Psalm 127 [read two times]: "Except the LORD build the house, they labour in vain that build it: except the LORD keep the city, the watchman waketh but in vain."

The first half of the message title in Akan, Gye Nyame, is also the first two words of the text in English. In either language it means "unless God." The rest of the Akan sentence is widely understood in a kind of Akan or Ashanti shorthand, which equals the full Bible verse: "Without God there is nothing. Unless the LORD builds the house, they labor in vain that build it." Our West African ancestors believed this, centuries before they ever saw a Bible, and they witness to it all over the place. They paint those two words on every taxi and every crowded jitney bus, and countless other places.

One of these two-word verses was painted across the top of the doorframe of a chapel on the beach. The fishermen prayed there every morning before they ventured into the dangerous waves in those little rowboats they had carved out of large logs. The (not always brief) prayer services which still often precede our public worship can no doubt be traced back to this tradition: Do not start anything important without asking God to bring it to success. Surely you don't even dream of seeing it come out well without having asked God to take control of it.

One Sunday afternoon, I rode with a deacon from one mission church to an even smaller and younger mission church to celebrate the dedication of a better place of worship. After we had filled the car a bit above capacity, there was a sudden silence. Before I could ask what the matter was, a fine teenager lifted his voice in passionate prayer for highway safety. They didn't travel an inch in that family without God. It was a profound lesson. In addition, the church we were visiting didn't drive a nail or lay a block without awareness of God's enablement.

This twentieth anniversary, we thank God for hammers, shovels, trowels, and the skilled hands that used them at no charge, whether they were members or just gracious neighbors. We even need to thank God for the denial of our first application for a building permit. Although we were crushed at the time, God knew that plans for a major highway in the future would cross right over the land we wanted to use. Today we thank God for making us find another and better building site. Thank you, Lord, for making *everything* work together for good (Romans 8:28)—even those building restrictions on structure and parking.

Our text goes on to declare that people who build without God are working in vain. Is that really true or just an outburst of religious enthusiasm? After all, the process of building is eventually a risk in one way or another, is it not? So why do God's California earthquakes destroy what were some of the finest of old church buildings and leave others standing? There are two ways to answer that.

The first answer is that some old structures are still standing even though they were made with wood or adobe. They were built to withstand the quakes God made, so that we could have oceans and mountains. We could not have dry ground and mountains without the tectonic movements underground that made the quakes. Unfortunately, some innocent, sincere Christian engineers did not study enough to see God's plan of creation, so the structures they planned fell in the storms and quakes. We cannot blame God when there are primitive peoples, and many wild animals, who seem to know more than top scientists know about when natural disasters are coming. These natives say God tells them, all of which suggests that God has a remedy for every one of our ills, and we have not accepted God's guidance to look in the right places. Maybe we studied war when we should have spent those billions studying peace, creation, and life and health.

The second answer about building in vain without God is much easier to see and understand. It boils down to breaking God's engineering rules, such as the shortcut house built on the sand in Jesus' parable. This house's falling was the effect. The most unsatisfactory part of this why of catastrophes is the fact that the major sinners in government and big business are not the major sufferers, in both the hurricane and the oil spill in Louisiana and surrounding states.

For example, in New Orleans, the largest and most concentrated damage to life and property was not due directly to Hurricane Katrina. It occurred in the part of New Orleans where the poorest people, largely African American, lived under the worst conditions. The flood that wiped them out was due to the weakness of the levee that failed to hold back the river. The millions originally appropriated to strengthen the levees in New Orleans went elsewhere to benefit far less endangered white people, for the profit of white people already rich. This is a classic example of building in vain and without either the blessing or guidance of God.

The oil spill is destroying wildlife in and around the northern end of the Gulf of Mexico, eliminating all hope of jobs in the seafood industries. It is the result of shortcut safety measures, breaking God's rules and obeying the god of the dollar. I know of a church which discovered an underground river on its site. Yet, within God's laws and with God's help, they managed to build a fine sanctuary on adequate footings built by God's laws.

One could say that the roughest waters in our church history were not underground but on the floor of some of our church business meetings. We had some members who for the moment were seemingly mean at almost every session. Thankfully, the storms did not last too long. Some other members earnestly and constantly prayed God's will, and God gave peace. We managed to navigate the stormy waters of incorporation and by-laws, building plans and permits, and financial need. By the grace of God, this sanctuary shows no signs of the storms. We did not labor in vain, because God was building our house, and many of us had sense enough to know that we only helped. These are details of which we need not be ashamed and which we must never forget. The smoke of petty battle clears away, and by the grace and power of God, we resume progress.

People and issues are inevitably human, and the best of human leaders dare not expect to exercise perfect control. If we have come these twenty years this well, surely God brought us. As the text says, unless God does pull all these things into a building, they labor in vain who try to build.

Of course, the tenor of our times will surely lead some to challenge this level of thanks to God. They ask, "Don't we officers and hard laborers get any credit at all?" Of course, we do get credit, but only after we face the fact that it was God who gave us the needed talents and God who worked all these egos together for good. God honors us greatly by counting us worthy to be used. Beware of the feeling that we are doing God a favor. We best rejoice in having a place inside the plan of God. Avoid the error of the little boy with the food-producing garden.

The story goes that when the boy's grandpa visited him, he insisted on showing Grandpa his garden. Grandpa was greatly impressed and patted him on the back, saying, "This is very good. The rows are straight, and the weeds are gone. You'll soon have some fine green beans. You and God have done great work." To which the child replied perkily, "Yeah, but you shoulda seed all those weeds when God had it by hisself."

The boy overlooked that it was God who gave him the strength and skill to plant and care for his bean crop. God made it grow. God even used the weeds to hold the soil together until planting time and the healthy tilling of the hoe. Everything else we do with the talents, tools, and materials that God gives us is like this. Gye Nyame. Unless God . . .

However, there are huge changes on every hand. Instead of raising our own beans, most of us today receive them cut, cleaned, and frozen. Machines put our automobiles together. We even drink plant-based substitutes for milk and study our Bibles with computer-driven aids. Of course, none of this is without God, who made all the materials and all the plans for our use.

To be sure, all of these changes require that we change our notions of what roles God wants us and our churches play. For instance, as a child I walked three-quarters of a mile to Sunday school and morning worship, and I thought nothing of it except on rainy days. With today's laws against discrimination in real estate, people may live fifty miles away and yet attend church every Sunday and during the week. Today, church ministries will have to adjust to this changing need, including the huge expense for land purchase and paving for parking. We dare not resent off-street parking laws, because "If you can't park 'em you can't save 'em." The church of Jesus Christ has to change ever more rapidly.

Only by such adjustments can Jesus' prophecy hold true today and tomorrow: "the very gates of hell shall not prevail against it" (Matthew 16:18). Unless we keep up with needs of the times, how can we believe God is building us? Look what God did a hundred years ago. There were laws against slaves reading, but poverty-stricken churches took care of that. As soon as they were free, they taught people to read. What reading was to them, computers are to us today. Reading was the key to decent jobs then; computers hold that role now. Apparently, nobody was afraid that God wouldn't keep on building through them and their church.

In those days churches sponsored orphanages and what we called old folks' homes. They were a major part of the vision, alongside schools. A facility for the very elderly had to have a house with multiple bedrooms and sisters who could cook, clean, and care. Today, a facility has to be first cousin to a hospital in space, staff, and equipment. All of this can be provided by all the God-built churches to which God gives the vision. It looks as impossible on the surface as schools did to the poor people whose offerings measured in pennies and nickels and dimes and even a few quarters. However, God was behind the project, and the churches kept it going until the law granted them rights to public education.

Orphanages are not that hard to replace, since loving foster homes and subsidized adoptions are better. God builds churches that see to it that the family of Jesus Christ is open and lovingly accepting of love-hungry children into their adoptive or foster homes. In fact, my wife and I had a doctoral student who stretched it even further. When the bishop of her African Methodist Episcopalian Zion church moved her from a storefront mission in the hood to a comfortable congregation in the suburbs of Washington, DC, she brought some of her most needy single-parent families with her. As part of the mission of the church that God built, these families found themselves mentored and helped by the so-called privileged members. This manner of mission is within the reach of many more.

This level of ministry no doubt seems outrageous to some, if not many. You say, "Most of us are not that far out of the hood ourselves, and you dare to propose such high demands and risks?" My answer is in agreement, but it is not as risky as the hut homes and tough towns our first teachers shared, in order to bring the three Rs to some of our most needy communities 130 years ago. Indeed, many of us were not terribly far from one of these most needy places when God told us that a church belonged right here, to meet our spiritual and multiple other needs, just twenty years ago. That is why God built this lovely, two-hundred-capacity church home.

Our ancestors are leaning over the balcony rails of heaven and rejoicing over the marvelous progress. We will be even more astounded at how much further God will help us build, given what we had to begin with. So often, we have thought we could not do, until we prayed and discovered that God said we can do, and we did. We cannot stop now!

In conclusion, please permit me to share with you the way I, at the age of five, learned and remembered our secondary text. It also concerns the endless endurance of the church of Jesus Christ. It is Jesus' commission to Peter on the Mount of Transfiguration in Matthew 16:18. It was a Sunday afternoon in the summer of 1924, and I was sitting on a bench of the First Baptist Church of Chillicothe, Ohio, with my short little legs sticking straight out. A congregation of illiterate ex-slaves had built this fine brick building. They each signed the Articles of Incorporation with an X. Nobody would have expected that church to have lasted very long. Nevertheless, it was going strong a century later, and that is what the visiting pastor was celebrating.

I was not greatly interested in the sermon, as far as I can remember, until the guest preacher started his illustration of the staying power of the church, against which hell itself could not prevail. The use of the h-word greatly enhanced my attention, since I hadn't been allowed to use it. Then the preacher recalled how, when he was a little boy, he heard dogs barking at the moon every night. He even gave us a remarkably accurate sample. I was really impressed. You see, I was also fascinated with dogs and really hung on every word after that.

He said that the detractors of God's church, especially First Baptist, were like the dogs, as they barked at the church especially during the earlier years. They had made cruel comments: "How can they operate a church when they can't even read and write? They belong back in slavery." Now the dogs were long gone, and the moon was still there. The preacher's closing celebration rejoiced that the church's detractors through the years are long gone, but old First Baptist is still going strong, standing as a landmark in Chillicothe's rich history. The gates of hell couldn't prevail one drop against it, and that was one happy congregation. Ministering fruitfully, always in God's will, they could do another hundred years and then some.

Unless the Lord builds the house, they labor in vain that build it. When Jesus Christ is the builder, the very gates of hell shall not prevail against it.

Amen!

4

YOUTH SUNDAY

AMERICAN CULTURE, heavily influenced by mass media, focuses unhealthily on appearance and styles. Over much of this, most youth have no control. Not only does this over concern apply to clothing and hairdos; it applies also to facial and other physical features. Teenagers in particular are overly sensitive about pretty countenances and hairstyles and the size and shape of their bodies.

Among African American youth, add a huge concern about skin color, hair texture, nose shape, and lip thickness. These features are especially damaging to self-esteem because these youth have no control whatever over their inheritance or their desirability in majority culture (that is, except the sort of surgeries that only a Michael Jackson could afford). This is all in the hands of the media and America's current ethnic majority, its middle and upper economic classes.

The African American desire for full social acceptance is frustrated at the deepest levels, with tragically damaging psychic results. This sense of failure to gain acceptance for one's appearance and ethnic identity prevails for all save a few movie stars, some top professional athletes, and other exceptionally high achievers in government, business, and education. However, the worst part of this issue is not yet mentioned or even known by most.

When people have low self-esteem and detest their own appearance, they are bound to have mixed feelings about the God who they believe made them that way. They do not dare face this inner reaction for fear of God's response, as if God would be insulted. Nevertheless, with or without openly facing the question of God's justice, the damage is done down deep. Many of our African American youth need to hear this sermon. In fact, the message is important for anyone questioning his or her looks and suffering from low self-esteem. The approach used here avoids cultural confrontation and supplies encouraging data. I first preached this sermon at a revival, with a youthful audience guaranteed by including the large youth choir after a brief regular rehearsal.

The preacher's behavioral purpose is to be used by the Spirit to motivate and spiritually strengthen the hearers' self-esteem, in relation to personal identity and appearance. The following moves may be helpful suggestions, after introduction of the need for self-esteem:

Move 1:   In awesome wonder consider with David God's detailed knowledge of David and us.

Move 2:   Consider in greater-than-usual detail the ways in which we are wonderfully made, as remedy for self-rejection (lack of healthy self-esteem).

Move 3:   Celebrate the certainty of knowing well our individual beauty as persons, even as the Scriptures detail Jesus' with parallels to every group. (Rev. 1:14-15, Sing "Fairest Lord Jesus.")

SERMON TEXT: PSALM 139:14
I will praise thee; for I am fearfully [awesomely] and wonderfully made: marvellous are thy works; and that my soul knoweth right well.

Am I Ugly? Am I Pretty?

In the 1960s, many African American youth suddenly declared that black is beautiful. They stopped processing hair and lightening skin to make them look more like white folks. They wore their hair in its natural state. It seemed a healthy trend indeed, but the self-esteem did not last very long. Little by little, folks went back to the barbershops and beauty parlors. They may have stopped using skin crèmes to lighten color, but if so, the difference was hardly noticeable. Fifteen years later, the few naturals who remained were widely interpreted as signs of either extreme radicalism or lower cost for hair care. Now one sees the cautious return of a slightly more disciplined design approach to unprocessed locks. They appear among a few avant-garde black intellectuals and other committed nonconformists and sensitive black nationalists.

Admittedly, these are risky generalizations. Speaking as a barber of naturals, and not a researcher, I have witnessed the torture of black self-rejection from a rather strategic position. The slogan about the beauty of blackness turned out to be a shallow fad. Its proponents were popular but never pure. Some of the most outspoken black radicals sought and found romance outside of the very beauty they declared. And in the case of unkempt hair, real beauty was never there to start with.

It is now high time that we revisit and reaffirm the beauty of blackness, but on the sound grounds of the Creator's equal distribution of beauty to all human beings. After all, God made each of us in his own image. King David, the psalmist, speaks and sings for all humankind in the words of the text in Psalm 139:14: "I will praise thee; for I am fearfully and wonderfully made: marvellous are thy works; and that my soul knoweth right well."

Now, let us reflect on our sermon title: "Am I Ugly? Am I Pretty?" Once again, our text: "I will praise thee; for I am fearfully and wonderfully made: marvellous are thy works; and that my soul knoweth right well." The great war hero, the king, is downright awestruck, as he says, at the way human beings are made and move.

Because beauty of appearance looms so large in our everyday culture, let us focus first on visible beauty. Of course, you are asking, "Who needs beauty talk in a spiritual revival?" I, of course, am happy to explain, particularly with so many youth here tonight. You see, people are spiritually sick who hate the way God made them. Everything God made was very good (Genesis 1:31), and that especially includes you and me. The first human beings were dark-colored. Besides, we are to love our neighbors as ourselves (Mark 12:31). All of this means we need to love all three—God, neighbor, and self—or love no one. Oddly enough, that means that we have to learn to love the way God made us, if we love God; it is a spiritual necessity.

David was a man after God's own heart (Acts 13:22), and that included David as a soul wide open to God's magnificence as Creator. David revered creation (Psalm 19:1). In today's text, he was in similar awe of his own physical self. He saw himself as "fearfully and wonderfully made."

Young people especially seem open to the wonder of the starlit sky. I was strangely touched by my eleven-year-old son as we camped under the stars on a clear night. He had a lump in his throat as he called attention to the beauty of the firmament. The boy was deeply moved, with no influence whatever on my part. Today's text would challenge us to be equally moved as we contemplate the birth of a baby and the beautiful and miraculous details of birth and daily life, regardless of color, or size, or age, or what Hollywood would call attractiveness. After all, secular beauty is in the eye of the beholder.

In the late 1930s, the all-male college I attended accepted more than a dozen students from West Africa. Seeing several of them lounging in the lobby one evening, some playful American organized a beauty contest—men against men.

More importantly, it was African men against American men, as the organizer no doubt intended. The criteria applied were African, and less than very dark contestants were adjudged unattractive. The local organizer got his laughs and made his point: beauty is in the eye of the beholder. That, however, is not my point: I agree with Genesis 1:31 that everything God made was very good, and that includes good-looking people, all of them.

If it happens to sound extravagant to say that all of God's children are beautiful, visualize all the babies you have ever known. See if even one of them was not outright adorable. God seems to equip them with countenances that reach right straight to your heart. Abused or abandoned, and otherwise helpless, they come to this world with a strange and lovely preparation for winning somebody's deep affection. Cold indeed is the heart that does not respond to the powerful attraction of a young baby.

It is somewhat the same with brides. With or without a gorgeous gown, given the countenance of one whose love is truly being fulfilled, the aura of beauty is awesome. The light of the human spirit is indescribable. At the beginning of my own sixty-four-year marriage, in 1944, I had the same experience when I gazed into the radiant countenance of my bride. I was moved to a point of tears of spiritual joy. My tears remained a secret, however, as the August temperature in Manhattan was so high that they appeared no different from the perspiration on my face.

The awesomeness of human life and its physical residence is not restricted, however, to drama such as these examples. How then can any believer say that any human being is ugly, especially oneself? What does one have to have to be born ugly and unhappy about it?

Features disliked in one place are handsome somewhere else, bought and sold for high prices. People with light-colored skin risk cancer, but pay for time in a tanning parlor. People with very thin skin and lips pay to have their lips supplemented with injections. When Salvador Dali glorified the protruding derrières of West African women, Parisian fashion adopted additions sewed into the backs of their best dress designs. This says nothing about the booming trend in bust extensions by bra or by cosmetic surgery. From thickened heels to tinted hair, people seem discontent with the way God made them. Consciously or unconsciously, this could mean they do not like themselves, and they do not like their Creator either. Alternatively, to soften it a little, they like prevailing, constantly changing styles more than the color schemes and outlines of God's handiwork. Either way, of course, we assume a combination with good health habits.

Who is ugly anyway? Why does it matter? For the despised peoples of the earth who have often had their self-images crushed by the culture of the power majority, the struggle to be pretty matters. Projecting the features of the majority as the standard for all pulchritude gives all who differ a rating of ugly. So this discussion matters because it calls for the healing of the broken-hearted (deeply depressed), to quote Jesus' commission (Luke 4:18). Real-life stories illustrate the possibilities for damage to self-esteem and the cure of self-rejection.

I was in the second grade when I experienced the cruelty of white *and* black bullies. The latter was worse. My marvelous father was unaware that his straight-across-the-forehead cutting of my hair, plus the squinting of my eyes, gave me a decidedly Asian appearance. My classmates taunted me with "Ching Chung Chinieman, eat dead rats; chew them up like ginger snaps." I had long since switched to grown folks' barber shops when I finally outgrew the considerable pain and frustration of trying to make my hair look acceptable. It was longer than that before girls my age began to think of me as an associate. There just was a tiny residue of this inferior feeling for years after that.

Frequent media news bytes report the tragic damage done by low self-esteem through reckless rejection of adequate food intake: suicidal diets. The dieter's condition is a disease, because it is amenable to medical advice and care. The condition most often begins, however, with extreme efforts to change the way God made an awesomely beautiful, healthy body. Fortunate is the patient who grows a gratitude for God's handiwork before it is too late to save it.

The chain of medication that ended in the recent death of one of the greatest entertainers of all time could very well have begun in the highly successful surgical efforts to erase his original physical image—the original appearance bestowed on him by God. This same Lord God gave him those matchless talents of which he had taken such good care. It is neither wise nor safe nor supportive of contentment to assume that we can improve on the main characteristics of God's human handiwork.

We turn now to a story of cure.

During the first night of one revival, we heard the text in Psalm 139:14. The youth had enjoyed the list of things other races pay to "be like us African Americans." I had alleged that full lips were more kissable than lips so thin the tooth profile shows. The positive value of this (now questionable) stereotype was learned two nights later. One of the associate ministers approached me before the service and said, "You really need to know how much you helped my twelve-year-old son the other night." I was delighted, of course, and curious. I asked, "How so?" He replied, "Well, you see, he used to walk around all the time with his lips pursed, like he was in deep thought. We always wondered what on earth he was thinking about, but we didn't ask. On Monday night, he burst through the door, smiling, 'Look! See! I have the most kissable lips in town!' He hasn't pursed his lips since. He doesn't feel the need to hide them anymore, I guess."

David's enthusiastic affirmation of being awesomely and wonderfully made is seldom considered in preaching text and worship. We are more likely to be found singing "Amazing Grace," where we celebrate ourselves as "a wretch like me," or "such a worm as I," as found in "Alas, and Did My Savior Bleed." The theological popularity of such overdone humility has died down, which is truly healthy for people needing far more self-esteem than they have been allowed. There is only a small recent recurrence of "total depravity" in most major theological circles. This overly negative notion of humanity, however, lives on in many hymns. It is widely used in the media and by some local ministries to manipulate audience support.

Fortunately, there are a few popular examples of a marvelously positive view not only of the natural works of God's hands but also the entire scope of human experience in the hands of God. Lyrics from a powerful song, sometimes thought of as a Western, mention the cry of a newborn baby, the familiar touch of a leaf, and the sight of a clear sky as reasons to believe in God. Everybody was once a newborn, and the awe with which we were then viewed only gets better as we add our contemplation of our unfolding into full-fledged adult persons.

Jesus himself partook of that unfolding (Luke 2:52). It goes from the grueling passage through the birth canal and all the way to the cross. His journey offers a certified example of abundant life, as he brought it (John 10:10), and as it can and should be, along with the suffering.

To the oppressed and cruelly mislabeled as unattractive, however, Jesus' life has a special and awesome relevance. The image of Jesus has to have specific human characteristics to be visualized at all, and not as an abstraction. These, as seen by John the Revelator, have Jesus with hair like wool and skin tones like burnt bronze (Revelation 1:14). These characteristics match those of people in Midian, on the northeast corner of Africa. This places Jesus that much closer to people of similar appearance. Sallman's head of Christ and all other Christ images are legitimate efforts to bring Jesus closer to specific people. What an atypical and unusual blessing, however, for people of color to be able to say, "But the Jesus of history looked more like us." There is no outright salvation in such, but it surely gives help in the places where the need for personal esteem is great.

David tops off his enthusiastic exclamation about himself as fearfully and wonderfully made with the glorious fact that his soul knows it "right well!" It is no mystery why he was so moved at how he was made. In physical size, he was probably smaller than his brothers were, since his father overlooked showing him to Samuel. His hands were awesomely dexterous. They were capable of victory in combat with lions as well as the giant Goliath. They could also play beautifully on the harp. Mentally, this same little brother was not only a poet; he was a brilliant military commander. He was also the uneducated but amazingly capable king, administrator of the whole of Israel. No wonder he was awed at himself as work of God's hands! He had every reason to be in awe of the giftedness that moved him from shepherd to monarch in one brief lifespan. He could easily see all of this because he was humble enough to look without blinding egotism.

If any should happen to desire to deny David's ecstatically joyous claim, he can hold fast even without earthly reaffirmation. "I may not always have been so certain, but now, hallelujah! I feel it in the very depths of my soul! What I once took for granted and paid no attention to is now a cause for unspeakable joy: this human form called my body is a piece of unbelievable genius, and I can feel it in the very bones of my soul!" whatever anybody else may think.

My ancestors would have expressed the same high gratitude for just being alive with traditional prayer rhetoric: "Thank you, Lord, my bed was not my coolin' boa'd, and my civer was not my windin' sheet." And, "Thank you, Lord, that you woke me up this morning, and I was clothed in my right mind." Or, "Thank you, Lord; I have the use of my limbs." Like David, my ancestors were outright joyous and awed just to be alive, and they claimed the further joy of simply being allowed to say so. Such sincere praise is healthy spiritually and full of healing. Praise the Lord!

Yes, I will praise you, O God, for I am awesomely and wonderfully put together; the way you made us is just plain marvelous, and my soul knows that real well.

5

MLK Holiday

THE ADOPTION OF Martin Luther King Jr.'s birthday as a national holiday is considered, all too often, as a political victory or defeat, depending on the person. Indeed, the honoree's political impact has indeed been very great on voting and elections. However, there is influence for which he has even greater and more lasting historic importance. It was King's introduction of higher ethical ideals, for example, that stirred up liberation movements among women and colonial nations around the world. Those ideals are still stirring, influencing further urgently needed improvements. It is his worldwide religio-ethical influence that I invite you to consider and lead in celebrating worshipfully.

Jesus' Sermon on the Mount sums up his personal guidelines for abundant life. Perhaps the least understood of these attributes is meekness. This is the same point on which Martin Luther King Jr. is most criticized by some friends. Thus, it is altogether fitting that this verse be explored on the day we honor his embodiment of this lofty human characteristic: meekness.

The sermon that follows was first delivered in Denver many years ago, and later in New York City. Three years later, we selected it for a Presbyterian service in memory of Dr. King held in James Chapel at Union Theological Seminary. The invitation included a request that it be preached in dialogue with my partner of sixty-four years, the now departed Rev. Dr. Ella Pearson Mitchell.

Since the notes for the first rendition were misplaced, we joined to rewrite the sermon from scratch as a dialogue. In honor of my beloved, it is presented here in dialogue format to maintain the flow. More importantly, it is to share the joint dynamics which had evolved.

As mentioned, the purpose of sharing all of the sermons in this collection is to serve, primarily, as a resource for ideas rather than a manuscript for performance. Of course, the reader always has the right to choose how to use this resource. It can help to know the following behavioral purpose and moves in consciousness.

This sermon's behavioral purpose is to seek to motivate fruitful Christian meekness in youth's pop culture of false pride. The moves drawn from the biblical text of "Blessed are the meek ..." might be as follows:

Move 1:   There is a rich model of meekness to be seen in the militant character of Moses' leadership out of slavery in Egypt.

Move 2:   Martin Luther King, Jr., and Gandhi are powerful models of meekness making important changes in everyday life in modern America and India, without violence.

Move 3:   We celebrate our blessedness in the fact that meekness has already inherited the earth in worldwide gender and racial breakthroughs, and political liberation movements in places like Russia and Germany (where meek Martin's "We Shall Overcome" was sung).

SERMON TEXT: MATTHEW 5:5
Blessed are the meek: for they shall inherit the earth.

The Awesome Meek

HENRY:
We are delighted to return to these sacred halls, left sixty-four years ago, and to this presbytery, from which I drew my marvelous partner. Our many ties here include a sermon preached across the street three years ago: "The Awesome Meek." We only wish we could have found the notes, not just the date. However, in cases like this, we usually avoid deep disappointment by assuming that the Lord is pushing us to make necessary improvements on the original.

ELLA:
Speaking of improvements, we were invited to do one called dialogue. We have explored this mode of preaching as one more resource for the greatly needed enrichment of the art of preaching in the United States. In other words, we prayerfully desire to be heard not as a performance or an act but as two preachers uniting in a serious effort to communicate the gospel in a fresh and compelling way, to reach the rapidly changing culture of our point in time.

HENRY:
Today's sermon-conversation requires that I briefly assume the role of an agnostic militant. He represents the kindly disposed host who question the nonviolent methods espoused by Martin Luther King Jr., whom, with his methods, we honor today.

My role shift is to spark our exchange. Since this is a sermon, the methods I challenge are stated in the form of a biblical text: "Blessed are the meek: for they shall inherit the earth." In my critical role, I want to know how in the world you can state and believe that meek people are blessed and happy. That is to say nothing of the fanatical notion that they shall inherit the earth. The question richly deserves a prompt answer.

ELLA:

Well, dear brother, if you have the time, I do gladly have some answers. In the first place, I am sure we are not on the same page with words like "meek" and "inherit." Let's define and exegete them first.

You are probably thinking of milquetoast-meek, but you could not be further from my definition. Meekness for you is shivering knees and quivering voices. Meekness is "Yassa, boss," and a bowed-down head with hat in hand, stereotypically known as Uncle Tomism. In your secular circles, meekness is avoiding opposing business prospects, no matter how ethically wrong they may be. It is supposedly good manners, whereby you never ever raise your voice or offend anybody with your deep convictions.

HENRY:

Mostly no, yet partly worse than your stereotype, this meekness is silent vulnerability to abuse and tragic deficiency in self-esteem. Meekness for me is, at worst, false comfort in a condition of ill-perceived powerlessness. It is the blind humility of a leader who persists in believing that his cruel oppressor has a conscience. How does your text speak now?

ELLA:

Okay! All right already! Maybe we are both into stereotypes. Let's get down to real people. I have always wondered about the reference to persons as "meek as Moses." Then I checked it out in Numbers 12:3. Moses was meekly ignoring the disloyalty and race prejudice of his brother, Aaron, and his sister, Miriam, concerning Moses' black wife. That, however, was not the whole story on meek Moses. He had already commanded powerful Pharaoh to "let my people go!" And he had successfully led his people out of slavery. That's the kind of meek I am talking about.

This meekness avoids ego trips and the waste of energy on petty issues of false pride. Meek people save their firepower for major issues. In the meantime, they forgive their enemies and thus save their own health. (The lack of forgiveness is hard on blood pressure, ulcers, and so on.)

HENRY:

Getting down to the important issues, your text says that such people are blessed and happy. I don't see Moses as all that happy and content. God punished him for his anger, and he did not get to set foot on the Promised Land. His meekness did not really pay off in happiness, now did it?

ELLA:

I can only say that what cost him so much was his *failure* to be meek before God. Even so, he had some marvelously fulfilling experiences in his meek mode, like standing on the dry side of the Red Sea in full freedom. That must have been a joy unspeakable. Nevertheless, of course, he did have little items on his record like the murder of an Egyptian.

HENRY:

This reminds me: Moses is really as much my hero as he is yours. Let's release me from my role as agnostic militant and pursue the text and the tribute to King in unison. Okay?

Looking back at your definition of meek, it may be wise to delete the "happy" and keep the "blessed" from the King James Version. One can be blessed and figure greatly in history without being what most people would think of as happy. "Content" is a better word to cover much of "meek" for modern purposes. Then we can apply it to Moses, Martin, *and* Jesus. If holding a major place in history can make you feel content—feel that one's life was well spent—then Moses, Martin, and Jesus were indeed blessed.

ELLA:

I'll go with that. Now let's move on to how this meekness works in confrontation with unprincipled power. King's opponents scoffed at a meek naiveté which assumed that there existed any major force whatever for good on this earth. How do you now defend against any such claim's basis in hard data?

HENRY:
Well, I have two kinds of responses.

One is the fact that not all meekness is as powerless as it seems. Reinhold Niebuhr used to insist that Gandhi's meek image may have held his followers together, but his millions of followers were a force to be reckoned with. The British Empire had due respect for the latent power of those millions, and India was freed. The royal government had no British blood to spare. The Montgomery bus strike had more than the Supreme Court in quiet reserve. It had the power to starve the bus company out of business, while black brethren and sisters stood meekly by to watch bus owners flirt with bankruptcy. Their meek refusal to step on a bus and pay a fare was a powerful weapon, if you please.

My second answer is that there is an unseen supporting spiritual force, such as that seen in the meekly endured crucifixion of our Lord. He had no hidden mob violence in reserve, as the secular world measures such. But look at the centurion. He was required to have the brute strength to subdue every one of his hundred-man squad. Yet this top sergeant's tough profession was no match for the countenance of the meek manhood that we sing about in the spiritual: "And he never said a mumbling word." This top kick gave up a life-long struggle for military promotions when he yielded to the meekness and cried aloud that this was surely the Son of God.

MLK is still chided for assuming the existence of conscience where there supposedly is none, but God is still God Almighty. Moreover, there is always an unseen ram in the providential bush, as it were. The powerful centurion yielded to the greater power of Jesus' meekness.

ELLA:

Let me share one of my favorite examples, drawn from the life of that prince of preachers, Gardner C. Taylor. Through no fault of his driving, a white man was killed in a collision in which Taylor was involved. Since it occurred in Louisiana, he was a cinch to be lynched. When the case came to trial, marvel of marvels, two white witnesses testified to Taylor's innocence! God set him free, to answer his call of Taylor to the ministry.

Whether or not one believes this kind of latent power to exist, seen or unseen, one certainly would not choose to use meek nonviolence as a military strategy. Nor would one dare to depend on meekness during any Alinsky-type violent organizational assaults on injustice. Regardless of the justice or equity at stake, Jesus' commitment to meekness and nonviolence was not negotiable. Nor was this commitment thought of as strategic or utilitarian in the minds of Gandhi or Dr. King. The trust was in God.

Meekness and nonviolence are the very will of God, as shown forth in the life of Christ. It appears in this same light in the civil rights movement under Dr. King. There was no attempt whatever to defend nonviolence as superior military strategy.

HENRY:

The text says, rather, that with or without the latent powers at work with Mahatma Gandhi and Martin Luther King, the meek *shall* inherit the earth. In other words, this presumably toothless host of peaceful demonstrators shall overcome all powers of opposition and prevail in due season in this planet. This is regardless of all apparent powerlessness, as this world reads power. And we are cold sober as we make this seemingly outrageous declaration. Indeed, we have scanned the history of humankind, and we dare to declare that we can document our claim with the results achieved in the limited number of historic situations in which meek and nonviolent disciples dared to follow God's strangely nonviolent will.

ELLA:

My favorite example of inheriting the earth drew my personal attention and enthusiasm when our younger daughter was blessed to receive a full scholarship to a prep school of the Quakers. I first met these historically meek folk (and their culture) up close there in the foothills of the Sierra Nevada Mountains. Then I traced them back to Philadelphia and on back to England. Strong traditions of meekness, gentleness, and simple lifestyles were encountered all the way.

I had known that Quakers opposed slavery, but the details of their lifestyle were amazing. All students at the John Woolman School learned to bake bread, feed chickens, milk cows, and cut firewood to keep boys' cabins warm. There were no exceptions for wealth. Distinguished semi-retired faculty lived like the rest, accepting pay of a dollar per year. This meek tradition was awesomely consistent.

So, also, was the way they had quite literally inherited the earth. This school was one of many well-supported and highly respected Quaker schools, mostly in the Philadelphia area. This support of expensive, high-quality schools was possible in part because of great Quaker wealth. I was in awe of the fact that Quakers loomed large in the Philadelphia banking world. Meekness, as promised in the Beatitudes, had not been without its meekly accepted inheritance of eventual huge rewards. No question about it, these meek did inherit the earth.

HENRY:

To push Jesus' startling statement to its ultimate extreme, we are reminded that Jesus did not say that the meek would inherit just the United States, or any other limited location; Jesus said it applied to the whole planet. It sounds briefly ridiculous until you remember that we have already mentioned the millions of India whose nonviolent meekness won them their liberation from colonial domination.

It is tragic that being meek was undermined soon after the death of India's quiet, gentle, and powerfully charismatic leader. Many of the indigenous leaders of the millions had never been convinced of the fact that meekness had won their freedom from British colonialism without bloodshed. In addition, there was even a peaceful unification of two great cultures and faiths. Unfortunately, here also was an opportunity for these local leaders to seize power for themselves. The division into India and Pakistan was the result, and the border tensions and wars have never ceased.

Mahatma Gandhi's witness did not die, however. There is a remarkably enlightening residue of his prophetic meekness found, of all places, in a magnificent movie portrayal starring Ben Kingsley. Few if any portrayals of meekness anywhere in the world are as graphic and arresting as Gandhi's handling of a degrading problem in primitive sanitation. The scene with Gandhi and the slop jar was most memorably meaningful to me, perhaps even more so because my own childhood home was similarly equipped.

ELLA:

Moving swiftly from this embarrassing candor let us look briefly at a more recent and amazingly miraculous victory for meekness at a national level. After twenty-seven years of unjust imprisonment, Nelson Mandela succeeded in the dissolution of a heavily armed and deeply entrenched system of apartheid in South Africa. There were no shots fired, and the takeover of control was without organized bitterness or massive revenge. There are still many wrongs to be righted and many Africans whose wounds are far from healed, but the process is still at work, and what bullets could not do for either side has happened and is still happening as the meek inherit the earth.

Let us conclude with an appraisal of MLK's unswerving commitment to meek nonviolence and his place (and that of Gandhi and Mandela) in the inheritance by the meek not only of this country but this whole earth.

Let us start with the rapidly diminishing memory of King's contribution to the well-being and moral integrity of these United States. Children in this generation are already unable even to imagine the everyday atrocities I endured as a child, or that my father was first allowed to vote at age eighty-four. You do not have to equal my ninety years to remember lynching and blatant inequality of teacher pay and pupil resources. We owe the success of the movement, as King directed it, not to riots and armed threats but to the meek acceptance of unjust arrests and hundreds of innocents cast into overloaded prisons. The task is not completed, but the human rights score in this country is unspeakably better than it was sixty years ago, and despite many recent setbacks. Not a gun or tank was necessary to get the vote or to equalize teacher pay. The quiet, yes, meek influence that did it all was from a catalyst named Martin Luther King Jr.

I just want to move on to the whole earth and the countries where, as in our black communities, whole governments used cruel official violence to enforce injustice. Yet they finally lost against a struggle with the meek.

Come with me to Berlin, with untold billions squandered on armaments to maintain division and domination. Families became brutally splintered. Hundreds of lives were lost in the effort to escape to freedom beyond that wall. Now look! The wall has come down, with no shot fired or any bomb exploded. When the wall was down, these people meekly and harmoniously sang with joy, as the crowds on both sides melted together across the ruins of the wall. Would you believe it? They were singing "We Shall Overcome," the hymn of the magnificent meek. The power of the powerless and penniless had proven irresistible. Blessed, indeed, are the meek!

HENRY:

Years ago, I heard a Chinese scholar and refugee extol the influence of Martin Luther King's ideals on the dreams and ideals of his generation of youth. He was speaking at a King memorial, and his testimony was for this occasion, but it was from his very heart. His participation, influenced by King, in the worldwide inheritance of the meek was done at great sacrifice but embraced without reservation—blessed indeed amid much suffering.

Equally moving was a testimony from the vice chair of Moscow's KGB. My wife and I were not there when this incident happened, but the memory of the published account stirred our very souls as we passed the headquarters of the cruel and unspeakably brutal Communist KGB, located in the Kremlin.

The memory stirred was about the visit to these offices by a group of nineteen American Christian church executives, pastors, and others. A few spoke fluent Russian. Conversation had no doubt drifted to the tortures of former years. An American pastor confessed his own overwhelming bad conscience from his sins as a U.S. Army intelligence officer in World War II. He concluded with his deliverance through Christ's forgiveness. Both he and the army general, who had once doubled as vice chair of the KGB, were in tears. He confessed to shedding such tears for only the second time in his life. Indeed, the entire group of Russians and Americans shed a flood of tears.

Instead of attempts to defend KGB excesses, the talk that ensued was about repentance and forgiveness, all at the request of spirit-hungry Russians. What the superior armaments had utterly failed to do had been achieved gloriously and unexpectedly by the meek and nonviolent. The hope of millions of Russian peasants, still oppressed under the yoke of Communism, was aroused and activated as they too sang their version of "We Shall Overcome" all over the country.

ELLA:

I tell you, the witness of history is awesome. The meek, the gentle, and the nonviolent *shall* inherit the earth. From India, to China, Russia, Mississippi, to anywhere else you care to mention, the meek *will* inherit what they are due. The swords *will* become ploughshares, and money once spent on munitions *will* build schools, hospitals, and churches.

UNISON:

The kingdoms of this world shall surely become the kingdoms of our Lord and of his Christ. And he shall reign forever! Hallelujah!

6

STEWARDSHIP SUNDAY

EVERY CONGREGATION has a budget, and with it goes the necessity of an every-member canvass for underwriting it with pledges. This, in turn, calls for a service of worship focused on Christian stewardship to launch the campaign for pledges. This should be a joyous celebration in tone, but often it is not. Laity and pastors try to put on a happy face, but underneath, they dread this annual exercise. This is not so much a matter of laborious detail as a problem of requiring a seemingly beggarly tone. There is a profound need for giving to be more joyous (2 Corinthians 9:7).

How dare we act as though we are doing our Lord a favor?

The sermon that follows makes an effort to merge sincere love of our Lord and his kingdom with sound awareness of the realities of finance and the family budget. In response to the presumably sincere challenges of many cautious Christians, this sermon offers the advice of the Lord himself as financial consultant and then the supporting testimony from contemporary experience in such biblical plans as tithing. This is not the same thing as the witness of wealthy stewards like Rockefeller, Colgate, or Kraft. These latter are not emphasized here as much as is often the case, because this plays too easily into the heretical trend of a theology of riches. The soundness of Jesus' awesome financial wisdom is a better model and basis for the stewardship of the more common members. Of course, the recent recession has made many more believers among the formerly top 5 percent. Many there are who have wished that they had heard and believed Jesus' word sooner.

I preached this sermon several times in my role with church extension in the 1950s. It was resurrected and enriched in the 1990s as a dialogue with my late pulpit partner, Rev. Dr. Ella Pearson Mitchell. The most memorable dialogue rendition was at a church where, unbeknown to us, the choir director had just completed a jail term for embezzling bank funds. For the amused hearers, and for us, it was an amazingly immediate validation of Jesus' appraisal of the trustworthiness of this world's financial institutions.

The sermon is here in still another version, in an imaginative dialogue with Jesus himself. The behavioral purpose is to move the members of the church to trust in God enough to enjoy their reasonable pledges in support of the churches ministries.

After the introduction of the sermon setting, the moves in consciousness are as follows:

Move 1:   Builds on Jesus' parable of the rich farmer.
Move 2:   Illustrates the instability of material things with examples from the real world.
Move 3:   Demonstrates the fallibility of human systems of finance.
Move 4:   Reveals and celebrates real-life promises of God in Matthew 6:33.

SERMON TEXT: MATTHEW 6:19-20,33
Lay not up for yourselves treasures upon earth, where moth and rust doth corrupt, and where thieves break through and steal: But lay up for yourselves treasures in heaven, where neither moth nor rust doth corrupt, and where thieves do not break

through and steal. . . . But seek ye first the kingdom of God, and his righteousness; and all these things shall be added unto you.

Jesus Christ, Investment Counselor

Please join me this Stewardship Sunday in a focused experience of imagination. It is a contemporary conversation with Jesus himself—a format given to me when I was meditating on how to be used of God to enhance pledges without the typical big beg.

In case you feel that you would prefer a conventional sermon, let me explain that this, too, is a serious message built on Jesus' model of narrative. Matthew, Mark, and Luke all report how Jesus used parables. These were imagined stories with powerful meanings. For instance, Jesus' most important story was about a prodigal son, with important meaning about the forgiving grace of God the Father. It was far more effective than a doctrinal lecture on the grace of God would have been.

Our story today is about a young pastor who consults with Jesus about raising the money to meet next year's church budget. Jesus' imaginative responses are based upon Jesus' own words of record, given in Matthew 6, in the Sermon on the Mount. [The dialogue presented is between a pastor and Jesus. You might dramatize your shift between characters by turning around or shifting from left to right.]

PASTOR:
Good morning, Lord! It is such a delight to see you first thing this morning!

JESUS:
I am delighted to see you, too, Pastor. However, you do look a bit anxious about something. Is there anything I can do to help you?

PASTOR:

You surely can, Lord. I'm not asking you to speak directly to my brother (Luke 12:13), but I would like to know from you how I myself might speak with power to the brothers and sisters of my congregation.

JESUS:

What is the problem?

PASTOR:

Well, you see, it's time to receive pledges for next year's budget. Only a very few people in the congregation are in the crisis of unemployment, or pension failure, or bankruptcy. However, almost everybody else is afraid to pledge even as much as last year. They are not poor or needy; they're just scared that they will lose their jobs, their homes or their excellent credit rating.

JESUS:

You put your finger right on it! They trust mostly in material things, and their concern for the kingdom is considerably less. All the while they are saving, yet they never feel like they ever have enough. You might want to give them fair warning with one of my old parables. It is the story of a rich farmer whose fields yielded more than they ever had before. He pondered the problem of storage space for a while, and then he said to himself, "I know what I'll do; I'll tear down my old-fashioned storage barns and build larger and more modern and efficient ones. When they are filled to capacity with all my tools and other possessions, I will say to myself, 'Soul, you have many commodities stored up for many years. Be cool; take it easy; eat, drink, and be merry!'" Nevertheless, he had no thought for the kingdom. Then God said to him, "You are foolish. This night shall your soul be required of you. Then whose shall all these things be?" Before he could even start construction, he died. Someone else enjoyed the wealth. That's how it goes with those who keep it for themselves. They are not rich toward God.

PASTOR:

I won't be able to tell it as well as you did, but that story should help people slow down and remember that they are not here on this earth with an unlimited contract. Every now and then, people do remember that they cannot take these treasured possessions with them, either.

JESUS:

Be sure that even when people live long and well, there are still lots of ways to lose the most precious possessions they have collected. In fact, they still have voracious moths eating holes in the best of clothes. These little bugs quietly and invisibly destroy pure woolen materials, regardless of all the precautions of the owners.

PASTOR:

I can tell my members what you have said, and I can surely back it up with my experience. The best suit I had ever owned still looks good, but only at a distance. In 2006, the moths had a picnic and selected my very best. What appeared to be a ball of white cotton lint on my left sleeve turned out to be the white lining shining through my *good* three-piece navy blue suit. If I had treasured that suit like some people treasure good clothes, I would have cried for days. As it was, Ella blotted it with ink and sewed it shut. Yet, it was never the same. The careful repairs were too obvious.

JESUS:

Moth and rust corrupt, as I have said, and the rust is deadly dangerous and far more expensive. It is so corrosive that your expensive steel bridges rust out, even though they are repeatedly repainted and maintained. The rust ruin on your country's pride and joy of superhighways would require incalculable billions to be brought to good and safe repair. Schools and other buildings have rust in their structure, and more and more buildings are declared unsafe . . . to say nothing of boats and automobiles. Should I continue the list?

PASTOR:
No, thank you, I have had more than enough on the moths, rust, and things of that sort. I shudder when I look back and realize how much all of us fail to observe the truth of that sound advice you gave so long ago in the Sermon on the Mount. I just remembered that lovely sedan we had in the early 1950s. The floor in the back rusted out from salt on the icy streets. We nearly punched through. They spray on an underseal nowadays, but no seal is perfect. Just think of how we, and millions more like us, treasured those cars!

JESUS:
Well, I am glad it all registers so well with you now. That bodes well for how effectively you will be able to communicate your concern. Do you want to finish looking at the other items of advice from that Sermon on the Mount?

PASTOR:
I hear you loud and clear. In fact, we need to hear the positive advice also. So, go right on with the thieves who break through and steal (Matthew 6:19).

JESUS:
Well, millions if not billions are spent in the pursuit of security, especially for money. And it has never been easy to frustrate clever thieves. In my day on earth, it was easy to break through unguarded walls. Technology today has brought huge changes. Today, you can open the heaviest steel safes given the time and equipment. Electronic timers can limit access to times when there are guards, but who is going to guard the guards? I need not mention the fact that thieves today have

keys to the buildings and the power to write checks. They are executives of worldwide corporations. Pension funds and the best of securities are compromised at the highest levels. One highly trusted fund manager has embezzled billions of dollars from nonprofit corporations. The details of the management of material things have changed greatly. Yet, nothing made or ruled by humans is eternal. All that is in a person's hands is subject to loss, both legitimate and unlawful. That does not suggest that there are no trustworthy managers. It only means that all ultimate love and trust can be given only to God. Therefore, lay up for yourselves treasures in heaven, where neither moth nor rust corrupts and where thieves do not break through and steal (Matthew 6:20).

PASTOR:

The vision is clear. The advice concerning all that we possess has not changed since you went on back to heaven. Of course, we can now reweave moth holes, but the styles change so rapidly that garments become obsolete and useless notwithstanding. Some banks stay afloat with aid from deposit insurance. Since human beings run these institutions, not one of them is infallible. Would you advise against savings and investments, then, to provide for old age?

JESUS:

Certainly not! The Bible is and always has been clearly supportive of savings, insurance, and pensions, once invented. The book of Proverbs used an ant as a model (Proverbs 6:6, 8). Paul told Timothy that those who do not provide for their families are worse than infidels (1 Timothy 5:8). Paul's word is clear in answer to your question: "Charge them that are rich in this world, that they be not high-minded, nor trust in uncertain riches, but in the living God, who giveth us richly all things to enjoy" (1 Timothy 6:17). It is one thing to love and trust riches, and quite another to love and trust God, regardless of possessions great or small, but sufficient.

Riches gained through honest, just, and humane means and applied to ends in keeping with the will of God are a blessing. As I summed it up, "Seek ye first the kingdom of God and God's righteousness, and all the things you really need will be added" (Matthew 6:33 [author's paraphrase]). This is a guide for investing in your life, and in all you are and have. All you need is promised, and no less.

PASTOR:
I cannot tell you how much I appreciate this plain and practical conversation on the way we invest our lives. I feel led to add some interesting testimonies of support when I share your advice on Sunday. The match between your timeless Word and today's realities is awesome. Thanks again from the bottom of my heart. Good-bye!

[Turn around and resume a monologue with the congregation.] Well, I am back with you now, dear sisters and brothers. Here are a few additional closely paralleled tidbits that I would like to offer you today.

The first comes from a *Wall Street Journal* article entitled "Can You Go Back?"[1] I used to wonder if any Wall Street investors ever thought of long-term investments in Jesus' visionary terms. Did any ever think of the Lord's work more than of their earnings in the bear market? Something of an answer came in the article. One brief quote said it all in bold letters: "Having it all isn't enough." Even if they were not cheated and robbed and earned what were fortunes in the market then, it still did not meet their real needs. "My life isn't going any place," said a forty-five-year-old male broker, living in a penthouse in Westwood. A fifty-three-year-old female television producer, caught in the same bind, stated her true predicament: "I'm separated from God."

Neither of them rushed back to church, but that is not my point. They had come to the profound awareness that they needed a spiritual relationship and nourishment far more than they needed to pay the light bill. Abundant income did not begin to fill the void. And they didn't seem too proud to let the world know how they felt. People like this are not far from the kingdom.

The second testimony comes from a family of two parents and three children, whose names I do not remember but whose insistent testimony I shall never forget. One Saturday afternoon, many years ago, I was rushing from the funeral of a treasured saint to the nearby airport and back to my parish in southern California. Suddenly a middle-aged couple detained me. They insisted that I hear what they had to say. They then repeated a story I had told in a sermon twenty years earlier.

The story began at a bus stop on the corner of Gilman and San Pablo, in northwest Berkeley. Dozens had walked up from the bay to catch the bus after visiting the horse track recently completed on the mud flats. An unusual number of the crowd were begging bus fare from whosoever would hear their plea. It turned out that every one of them had gambled his or her last dollar on a horse and, of course, lost. I noticed that although all these beggars had lost all they had, none complained. The uniform witness of every one of them was, "I wish I had had just two more dollars to bet." This had an effect on me, and I put it in a stewardship sermon: Christians need to be that anxious to give their very last, like the widow's mite (Luke 21:2).

In fact, the beggars at the bus stop are excellent examples of church members who are hypercautious about pledging to the church, all the while pledging to pay monthly for cars, houses, phones, and electric power. It could be more than startling to scan their lists. How strange indeed to realize how low God and kingdom are prioritized. Then they dare to pray, "Give us this day our daily bread."

This couple, after hearing the sermon, had taken it seriously. They prayed, meditated, and committed themselves to tithing, on the spot. They felt they had to share with me how they took the story and how God had blessed them ever since. They just had to thank me. All their children had finished college debt-free. They had paid off their mortgage and were driving their first new car. All because they, like the gamblers, wanted to give more, and still did. I tried not to let them see the water in the corner of my eye, but I am still rejoicing over their testimony.

Afterwards, my wife and I reflected on their testimony with joy. Regardless of the low salaries we had accepted and the tight places we had squeezed through, one of our two favorite verses was and still is that same text: "Seek ye first the kingdom of God, and his righteousness, and all these things shall be added unto you" (Matthew 6:33).

We never thought of it as bargaining with God, and neither had this couple. Nevertheless, we still say we wish we could give more, and if we ever get it we will, whether in life or in death. Hallelujah!

Note

1. Lisa Miller, "Can You Go Back?" *Wall Street Journal*, April 10, 1998.

7

WORLD MISSION SUNDAY

IN TODAY'S WORLD OF innumerable huge changes and shifts, no field is more in transition than world missions. In the century recently closed, the face of world missions has altered so radically and so rapidly as to require a complete redesign of attitudes, motivations, and missions involvement. While many will mourn the loss of paternalistic challenge, the whole world needs to rejoice in the limited progress toward a planet of equalitarian nations and peoples. As far back as the Laymen's Inquiry of 1932, it was clear that missionaries must be sent to reach across rather than down to people. Additionally, the entire missionary enterprise must cease cooperating with colonial domination and international economic exploitation. Even with the process of change launched nearly eighty years ago, there is still much to do.

Homiletically speaking, the lengthy sermon text readily organizes the sermon. The text's behavioral purpose is unmistakable, and the passage invites word-by-word expository treatment. For timing of impact, the text's built-in celebration offers a powerful and fitting conclusion. The challenge in writing this sermon is to find ways to make each traditional point come alive as a move in consciousness. In other words, rather than to offer the simple meaning of divine commands, the approach is twofold. One is to inform the hearer of current exciting conditions. The other is to make the mission picture so plain and enticing that the hearer will feel called to participate in the modern internationally inclusive church, possibly under a variety of programs, building a worldwide church/family in Christ. This call is the behavioral purpose of the sermon: to move the hearers to do Christian missions gladly and in keeping with the changes in today's world. The moves in consciousness are:

Move 1: Go now into the risky, fast-changing world.

Move 2: Go into ALL of this known world, as a family.

Move 3: Teach and empower them in everything Christ has commanded.

Move 4: Go in the unfailing certainty of Christ's ever-blessing presence.

SERMON TEXT: MATTHEW 28:19-20
Go ye therefore, and teach all nations, baptizing them in the name of the Father, and of the Son, and of the Holy Ghost: Teaching them to observe all things whatsoever I have commanded you: and, lo, I am with you always, even unto the end of world.

The Great Commission

My sisters and brothers in Christ, happy World Mission Sunday! There is a deep and abiding joy in sensing that today we join millions around the world in prayer and worship, slightly divided only by the oceans and the time zones, yet united in Christ!

Today, we remember and rejoice in Jesus' Great Commission to his church, that it go out into the world, teaching and baptizing them in the name of the triune God, Father, Son, and Holy Spirit. In the midst of it all, we sometimes shudder at the thought of giving that size of serious assignment to a task force of only eleven inexperienced and mostly illiterate men. They had no budget, or equipment, or means of travel. Today's huge church has come a long way since its inauspicious beginning. But today's rapid rate of change would suggest that we will have far less future time in which to adjust to the shock and burden of awesome changes in every facet of life and faith.

Here are some of the most obvious swift shifts.

Some of the receiving mission churches overseas today are stronger than the sending churches here. They need to have a place to launch their own missionary projects, but there are no untouched mission fields left. Any visit to Sunday worship in the Caribbean Islands may cause mainland Christians to wonder, "Why on earth do these people need missionaries? They sing far more hymns and recite more Scripture than we do, and they obviously enjoy deeply spiritual worship." Their kids behave in church. This is true also in many places in Africa and Asia. It is almost as though some religious bodies regret that there are no more easy-mark pagans left for them to look down on in ministry.

What is true of worship in the West Indies is also true of Muslim family life in the West Indies and in other traditional societies. The average child is obedient and studious. Muslim law enforces the strict sexual morality of Muslim society. In Cairo, we saw hotel desk clerks refuse a room to an unmarried millionaire couple from Sweden. The clerks defended their refusal with the fact the Cairo police inspect hotel registers some time during every night. Imagine the embarrassment of American missionaries when they read of the behavior of some famous American figures of televised worship.

Supposedly uncivilized countries once welcomed American and European commercial interests, which came in on the heels of the missionaries, bringing the development of resources and raising standards of health and education. They also brought the basic skills and requirements for newly developed self-governments. Soon after, the blessings of health and education observably appeared tied to greedy exploitation. We saw the withdrawal of our welcome at its worst.

A West African banker, son of a Protestant missionary from Jamaica, had royally entertained my family and me, during a visit to his country. We enjoyed the hospitality and reveled in the notion of a black participant in international finance. Hardly a month after we left, a revolution erupted. Among the first to be brutally slaughtered, to our horror, was our former host. Suddenly, we were sensitized clearly to the kinds of issues that have restricted activities and even closed the doors to missionaries in many places in recent years.

We dared not regret that the gospel had been so widely communicated and thousands saved. Surely we dared not rejoice in the bloody methods of the revolution. We simply were compelled to face the fact that the days of stereotypical, reach-down, patronizing missions are long since over. They whom we still send, if any, must now find God's will in the effort to reach, teach, and help develop accepting nations and churches on equalitarian terms. Meanwhile, we must be doing what is often called cleaning up our act.

The gospel always was and always will be good news, but the ways we witness to it are in the process of huge changes to fit into the awesome shifts confronted by missionaries and by all humanity in this era of still more rapid change in technology and human history. The future is still as bright as the promises of God, with the obedience of humankind.

First of all, then, as we have just observed, our Lord's great commission will prevail only as we face reality and move on. The utter seriousness of Jesus' sweeping commission can be seen more clearly when we realize that these were his last words on earth. Our seriousness, however, must match that of Jesus.

Thus far, we have focused on the problems of rapid change and the errors of attitude that have beset the worldwide efforts of Christian churches. We have been thinking primarily of the Protestant bodies, and of Orthodox, Pentecostal, Anabaptist, and other traditions not within the Roman Catholic Church. It is time now to merge Jesus' last word with our best insights, to humbly seek God's will in building a worldwide family of Christ. The church of Jesus Christ for tomorrow must be characterized by Christian love and mutual support, using our gifts from God in ministry *with* all fellow believers everywhere.

Let us look now at the twenty-first century, at a positive vision to which the Great Commission calls us. The first ministry to which we are called seems still to be teaching: "teaching them to observe all things which I have commanded you" (Matthew 28:20). Whether in the pulpit, classroom, or humble abode, we must still be teaching, learning, and growing. Moses had no television and other teaching aids, but his word still holds. Be sure to chat about the Law (the Word of God) at every opportunity (Deuteronomy 6:7), in the street and in the bedroom, and wherever. This surely applies to mission ministry abroad, as well as witness at home.

For Moses, this was the principle of countercultural saturation, practiced to offset the huge attractions of Canaanite cultivated foods and drinks, colorful linens, and comfortable living. It took every possible moment of influence to keep the faith alive another generation among these traditional tent dwellers, berry pickers, and wearers of animal skins. Our similar predicament is as overwhelming today as it was then. The good news is that Moses' concentration of warm, casual teaching is as effective today as it had been when used by the Jews for centuries. We have supplemented it with modern media. Moses knew all too well that a faith style of one's own needed to be supported 24/7 by the entire extended family. This was their only hope of not being swept away in the low morality of the Baal-worshiping majority.

Our Jewish sisters and brothers have maintained their identity and their rich religious tradition these more than two thousand years. They have held against minority status and unthinkable persecution. It was because a goodly host of Hebrews has strictly followed this rule of Moses regardless of overwhelming opposition. Their witness as a body of believers says to us that what Jesus commanded is not impossible, regardless of how difficult it may seem.

Likewise, African American slaves screened out the heresies of masters and overcame the handicaps of legally enforced illiteracy and restrictions to worship, to embrace a Christian counterculture with awesome authenticity. Their memories were better than printed pages. Their traditional inheritance of word power and narration skills in teaching methods may yet help save the Euro American pulpit from increasing futility.

Here again is sufficient evidence, starting with Black Harry, Bishop Asbury's enslaved servant. His preaching drew larger after-crowds than the bishop's original audiences. The powerful tradition continues through Charles A. Tindley to Gardner Taylor and Martin Luther King Jr. There has been continuous preaching and teaching used by the Spirit to bring about changes in the course of human history. This is another way of saying what the commission calls for in "teaching them to observe all things whatsoever I have commanded you" (Matthew 28:20).

Again, I say, it seemed utterly unthinkable when Jesus told us to teach the whole world, but it looks lots more plausible when you contemplate all the resources Jesus has. Truth be told, the total worldwide resources are no longer on reserve. One is the literal arrival of the time when "there was no more sea" (Revelation 21:1). In other words, one can travel so easily from continent to continent that there might as well be no more oceans in between.

Recently I ate dinner as I left London at six, only to arrive in Los Angeles in time for dinner at six, having passed over the North Pole. Nevertheless, we are called and commissioned to witness with sisters and brothers in every place we land. Moreover, the witnessing goes both ways. No longer is China or New Guinea an idea or an abstraction. It can and should be real people, whose countenances we have beheld in person and kept in mind as we pray for them.

Since our overseas guests may be veteran Christians, we may be receiving more faithful witness than we give. The day is past and gone when we are always the senior saint. There may be no equality of worldly things, and our guests may even decline to receive our gifts. That may only mean that they may offer the better contribution to our encounter. In any case, the point is that the line of communication between is eye level, not moving up or down on either of us.

The word "mission" is no longer a one-way sending; it is a family in Christ, which goes in both directions. When planning a multipurpose vacation, one can enrich it by remembering the kinfolk in Christ, not all of them, but at least those in reach, whose membership has become a family tie in Christ. It applies to the whole year, like blood relatives. I have seen children and youth who grew up feeling just that kinship. They had aunts and uncles in Christ in places like Haiti, reservations in Arizona, and Zaire (Congo).

I saw this when hosting missionaries on leave, and on the typical itineraries. In town after town, there were warm, even tearful, greetings. It dawned on me that these people supported overseas and domestic ministries because there were people over there with whom they had living relationships. It was blood kinships in some cases, but the bond was always in Christ.

Whether or not we call it missions, the point is full and equal standing in the family of the church of Jesus Christ. Traveling groups of members from the same congregation have doubled the enjoyment. It was still more fun when we had study classes on the country and the mission to be visited, and a session on how and what to pack for the trip. I cannot forget the laughter when my wife and I unpacked each one of our small bags for a demonstration at Trinity in Los

Angeles. People thought it was a magic trick, there were so many garments dramatically withdrawn and displayed from those small bags. All of this was part of the fun, but more important was the spiritual richness, plus the bonding with new sisters and brothers in Christ in Zaire. What an unforgettable vacation! What a wonderful introduction to the worldwide mission of the church of Jesus Christ!

For making the mission come alive as a worldwide family in Christ, the most encouraging plan I have heard of was the dream of a pastor in Virginia. The church sponsored an African student in seminary many years ago. When he had returned home to answer his call to a church, the church in Virginia decided to invite him to preach a revival. His own church choir had planned to join him. Unfortunately, the death of both pastors ended the dream. But I still treasure the dream and hope to see it come to life again someday.

We conclude with the most rewarding aspect of the mission; it is included in Jesus' words in the Great Commission: "and, lo, I am with you always, even unto the end of the world" (Matthew 28:20). Of course, this is a spiritual presence, but it is manifest in concrete ways. For instance, one of the most blessed and indeed enviable groups of young people I ever encountered were the MKs in my seminary classes. They were up-to-the-minute informed on happenings all over the world. They had Phi Beta Kappa keys from the most respected schools and aced most classes without obvious effort. They were warm and friendly, with attractive personalities. They were never arrogant about their high achievements. One of these apparently effortless geniuses was the class valedictorian, of course. When health issues moved him home from an overseas mission, he spent the rest of his career as an Ivy League chaired full professor. You knew it all along, but I will tell you anyway: these super breeds of students were all missionaries' kids. They were offspring of a turn-of-the-century crusade of youth set on winning the whole world for

Christ. Their parents had left all to save the world, and they had taken their kids with them whenever possible.

If, as I believe, to succeed in raising gifted, dedicated children is the greatest possible reward, then this is what came from Jesus' promise: "Lo, I am with you always, even until the end of the age." No matter what hardships there might have been, the ever-present Lord got them through it and made it all well worth their while—and more.

Jesus still says, "Carry the gospel of love everywhere, and live it, and you'll be unspeakably glad you did what I commanded you to do, because I'll stick with you to the very end" (Matthew 28:19-20, author's paraphrase).

8

COMMENCEMENT, CHAPEL, AND OTHER ACADEMIC ASSEMBLIES

THIS SERMON IS FOR an academic gathering, usually with the understanding that it is either church-supported or private but not tax-supported. There are some famous exceptions where schools are also partially tax-supported; Pennsylvania has four such: Pitt, Penn State, Lincoln, and Temple. Sermons are still acceptable at the assemblies of all four. You may wonder, "What's the concern? Don't all colleges and universities have chapel services?" The answer is no. In fact, even in institutions where sermons are requested, there are still concerns about offending members of certain faiths. Pennsylvania's Lincoln University was founded in 1854 and supported for most of its history by Presbyterians. Now its chaplain has to lead worship acceptable to an amazing selection of faiths, including several Muslims. She or he must also communicate with those with supposedly no faith at all.

All of this leads up to the fact that today's choice of texts quietly reaches out to three traditions. I have preached recently from this verse, as found in Mark 12:30, in the mouth of Jesus. I now have the option of adding the comparable words from the Moses tradition, as found in Deuteronomy 6:5. Both the four-word emphasis and the title, "With All Thy Mind," refer to the same original indivisible human being. This, then, addresses not only Christians but also the various branches of Jewish tradition, and, to a lesser degree of loyalty, millions of Muslims.

This is not a rigged unity of thinking and belief; it is a natural consensus, drawing on the sharing of the same early roots. The concept of "heart" is still where it was then: the center of feelings and emotions. We all know the physical heart is not the literal locus of feeling, only the place all feelings or emotions register response. Notwithstanding all medical wisdom since Moses and Jesus, we are still unanimous about the heart as the center of feelings. In addition, our emphasis on mind has some commonality with Asian religious meditation. So we can innovatively design a sermon with freedom and creativity for reaching and touching virtually everybody, whether student, staff, or faculty, and even atheists, who just might have curiosity.

The focus of this sermon's behavioral purpose is on moving hearers to love God with the entire reflective mind. It is implied by all three major "book" religions (Hebrew, Muslim, and Christian). The full verse of the sermon text includes the three key words: heart, soul, and might. These covered their total known person. With the Greek word for mind, the New Testament reflected far greater emphasis on thought and reason, but it was not raw new meaning. Thus, without non-Christian resistance, there evolves a most appropriate behavioral purpose for an academic sermon/address. The moves in your sermon are filled with your real-life illustrations of:

Yes, you can and actually do love with your mind.

Move 1:   Our minds are most freely drawn to what we love, whether good or evil.
Move 2:   We can build good thought habits supporting our love by what we read, watch, and discuss.
Move 3:   Loving God and God's wisdom and truth with our minds leads to great blessings to our communities and abundant life for ourselves.

SERMON TEXT: DEUTERONOMY 6:5
Thou shalt love the Lᴏʀᴅ thy God with all thine heart, and with all thy soul, and with all thy might.

SERMON SUPPLEMENTARY TEXT: MARK 12:30
Thou shalt love the Lord thy God with all thy heart, and with all thy soul, and with all thy mind, and with all thy strength: this is the first commandment.

With All Thy Mind

Today, I invite you to what must seem to college students to be a strange activity. As you examine the title of my talk, the "thy" suggests that it must have something to do with the King James Version of the Bible. Also, freshman English will tell you that "With All Thy Mind" is just a prepositional phrase, which tells you that somewhere there must be the rest of a complete sentence to go with it. So you feel that I must be polite, and do what's right, and give you the rest of the sentence. "Don't leave us hanging." Okay! That's fair. I will start by reading two texts.

The first is from the Mosaic law from the Old Testament [read aloud]: "Thou shalt love the Lᴏʀᴅ thy God with all thine heart, and with all thy soul, and with all thy might" (Deuteronomy 6:5).

The second is the same, except that it adds a fourth modifier, "with all thy mind," and comes from the mouth of Jesus rather than Moses [read aloud]: "Thou shalt love the Lord thy God with all thy heart, and with all thy soul, and with all thy mind, and with all thy strength: this is the first commandment" (Mark 12:30).

This is not a language lesson, but you need to know this much: Although in Moses' day there was no Semitic word for mind, it was included in the understanding of heart.[1]

Therefore, both verses, Old and New Testament, are telling us, along with heart and soul, to love God with our minds—in fact, with our whole minds.

So now, I hear a wise sophomore objecting, "You love with your heart, and you think with your mind. What's this about loving with your mind?" So I say, "Joe Blow, you're right, but so is the Bible when it speaks it more than once, and especially in the mouth of Jesus. Let me show you how. It's not hard to understand, once you look at it carefully."

In the first place, we love most the person to whom our mind turns most often. We do not plan this thinking time; it just happens. We were not concentrating on anything or anybody in particular, when up pops her (or his) sweet countenance uninvited. Psychologists call it a sample or example of free association. I call this example love.

You do not need a stopwatch to deal with mind time. Large blocks of time are everywhere in human life. For instance, an ordinary fellow sees and chats with an attractive secretary quite often in an eight-hour workday. When he arrives back at his home, he is fully bushed. He takes off his shoes and lets the television news put him into dreamland. Then he chats at dinner and between football quarters, and he returns to dreamland. His mind focused on the office worker at least four times as much as on his wife. Is it any wonder that there are so many divorces? Unintended love may jump into your free association time, if you happen to leave the door to your mind wide open.

For sixty-four years, my wife laughed as she relayed to me the complaints of her lady friends: "He talks about you all the time." Well, that was because I was thinking about her quite often and was certainly not embarrassed by the fact. I pled guilty. In fact, I did not plan it that often, but the "girl" was just plain and simply on my mind. I couldn't help it! Wouldn't you call that loving with your mind?

If Joe wants to know how you love God with your mind, the answer is easy. You just think about God and all the things that pertain to God's providential care in your life. You pray and meditate and talk about God and think seriously about what you might call the will of God for your life and for your community, as part of the kingdom of God.

I can tell how much you love God by reading your checkbook or your list of reading materials. Jesus said, "Wherever you put what you greatly treasure, that's where your heart is" (Matthew 6:21, author's paraphrase). This is also true of the time you spend reading. You cannot love God and read only the *New York Times* and *Sports Illustrated*. I flunked that test for decades, before I got to where the Bible is what I read first most mornings (except when I read in my seat on any early plane).

Your choice of movies, television shows, and sports events tells a lot about where your mind is, as compared with your worship time, private and public. What kind of movie, show, or other event is it? The answers to these questions will tell what your tastes are and what your hearts and minds love most enthusiastically. In the abundant life of faith, it is not all or either, but where the majority is, and what comes first.

I sat in the pulpit with the pastor for a 7:30 Sunday morning worship. As I scanned the congregation, I was greatly impressed by the strong male majority. That was rare indeed, and I complimented the pastor on his effectiveness with men. He thanked me, but he said this wasn't typical. These guys were worshiping early so they would be free to go to the Super Bowl, or at least to watch it on television for the rest of the day. Can you guess which part of the day they enjoyed and loved the most with their minds?

Now, of course, there are other angles. You may read medical texts ten hours a day if you plan to glorify God and heal the neediest. Nevertheless, you cannot keep your faith readings at third-grade level and study everything else as a postgraduate. When people feel no challenge in their learning, they drop out altogether. I am inclined to suspect that failure to keep up in the love of God with the mind means more love for degrees and future professional fees than for thoughtful time with God.

Just to be sure I do not sound anti-intellectual, let us consider the fact that God is the Author of all truth and data, Lord of human history. Thus, in loving God with the mind, we are not limited to reading the Bible and related books. The more we know about calculus, the more we can stand in awe of God, who made it. Furthermore, we can express our love for God by our highly informed witness to God's truths. That's what the apostle Paul did in Acts 17:28. Being well read, he could quote ideas about God already believed by Greek scholars. This prepared the way for the gospel of Christ. The bridge was, "as certain also of your own poets have said."

My following witness happened in 1936, long before tsunamis made us all aware of the very deep movements underground. My twelfth-grade teacher stirred and stimulated me during a physics class to unspeakable levels of loving God with my mind. It was simple, done with a drop of water. He held it up and asked what happens if you heat it. We said, "It would expand." Then he asked the same of lowered temperature. We said, "It would contract. It's a law of physics." He pressed, "Are you sure? What if it went below 32 degrees Fahrenheit?" We were embarrassed and clammed up. We knew ice was expanded water; it floats. He responded to our silence with, "It's an exception to the rule, isn't it? What would happen if it weren't for this exception?" When we took the Fifth, he explained how springs, oceans, and rivers would freeze hard at bottom, closing the aquifers and other passages below the surface. It would stop the heat exchange, leaving earth unbearably cold in winter and unbearably hot in summer. We could not live here except for this break in the pattern.

Another drop of water appeared now. It was in the corner of his eye, as he said he could not say how this exception came about, since this was a public school. He didn't have to say it; I already had a drop in my eye and a lump in my throat. My spiritual joy at age seventeen was unspeakable.

Let us be clear about loving God with the mind. No matter how learned one may be, this does not justify arrogance. Quite to the contrary, increase in knowledge and wisdom fosters deep humility. The circumference of our body of knowledge expands as our wisdom develops. Thus, the more we know, the more we are confronted by the outside edge—by the infinite mass of the unknown. In other words, the more we know, the more we know that we do not know. I have been fascinated by the fact that much of the most useful advice handed down to me came from people who didn't have a full eight years of public education, much less high school or college. A school janitor—a deacon—critiqued the trial sermon I delivered as a college sophomore. It was easy to see just how sound his critique was. I have followed his advice ever since, and it has always been justified by the results.

Howard Thurman, a truly great preacher and theologian, often used to introduce profound truth by ascribing it to his illiterate, ex-slave grandma down in Florida. For her there had been no schools, but she loved the Lord with all her mind. The Lord, who is no respecter of persons or degrees, gave her equal capacity and crowned her best efforts with brilliant insights. She loved the Lord her God with all her mind, and that made it easy for the Author of all truth to bless her mind with deep insight.

I trust you will pardon reference to my family, but I feel led to share an example of God's mental enrichment as open to more than old folks. Our daughter probably had in mind no such comparison with ancestors. We saw it happen with her when she was in law school. Her friends questioned the wisdom of her presence at Sunday worship. They knew she had to plead a case in moot court the next morning. She surprised them, and it surely surprised us, when we heard that she had replied, "All the more reason for me to be here. I've done what I could, but I need the Lord's help."

Well, she must have gotten it. After class, the instructor complimented her with, "You use the English language as if you had invented it." In the conversation that followed, it came out that she was a PK (preacher's kid), to which the teacher said, "I should have known it." My point is that the love of God had not only moved her from study desk to worship; it had already filled her growing years in the parsonage with a natural grasp of the language. The teacher felt he should have detected it, because he had had so many other PKs who also had a grasp of the language because of their similar experiences.

This experience suggests unavoidably what might easily be mistaken as a sales pitch to "love the Lord your God with all your mind and you'll be blessed beyond all you might ask or think." However, love for even this purpose is not love; that would ruin the whole relationship. Love does not seek reward for itself, not even when the Lord God is the one loved. Notwithstanding, I dare not close this message without confessing that the most constant benefit of loving God with all your mind is joy. Nothing gives deeper and more lasting joy than using all of your mind and your voice in the love and praise of God.

God is pleased with our praise, but God does not need it. We need the joy and peace of loving and praising God, and using all our talents and intellects to do it. There is no other endeavor on earth which symbolizes the fulfillment of the individual and harmony with others quite like choral music. Besides, it brings a healing happiness to both body and mind. In fact, I am moved whenever I recall the Ebenezer Choir's rendition of Beethoven's 150th Psalm. More than seventy years ago, I had been ecstatically joyful just to get to practice it with the college glee club, three nights per week after dinner. It had moved me deeply as a sophomore, with those vigorous harmonies challenging everything that had breath to "Praise ye the Lord!"

As I joined the bass section under my breath, tears rolled down my cheeks, and I could not check the overwhelming awareness that this was almost like practicing for heaven, or as close as we will all ever get in this life. Such exuberant, vigorous praise, employing all existing harps and horns and percussion instruments, plus everything that has breath, is for eternity.

Meanwhile it is well to close out here on the love of the Lord our God with our minds by a stop at the nearer end of the worship spectrum. Aunt Jane an' 'em used to sing it, and we still do. It is what we call a spiritual [singing out]: "Woke up this morning with my mind stayed on Jesus."

Note

1. Craig A. Evans, *Mark 8:27–16:20*, Word Biblical Commentary 34B (Nashville: Thomas Nelson, 2001), 264.

9

WOMEN'S DAY

IN ALL OF CHRISTENDOM, it is probable that the most preva-
lent imbalance and inequity is that between female and male.
Congregational and denominational authority and recognition
are allotted, in blatant disproportion, to a male minority. In a still
great majority of cases overall, the choices for church leadership are regardless of gender proportions of support, talent, or
level of commitment. To top it off, the culture at large and an
apparent majority of adult women support this system. Justifi-
cation for such support may be the fact that the militant female
minority is viewed all too often with the kind of contempt re-
served for ultraradicals. Powerful female advocates are the exception, not the rule.

At first glance, this sermon appears quite appropriate for a
typical Women's Day service; however, even the most diplo-
matic treatment of these texts will inescapably make a few critical
comments about men. However, this is an unusual opportunity
to attract men with the analysis and humor of this fresh angle
of lay-level Bible study. For the women there is the frank facing
of the fact that wives often assume their identities based upon
the description of their husbands.

Please understand this is to be a well-deserved and positive
glorification of churchwomen, not a critical tirade about men.
One never wins frontal attacks on the well-established customs

of a culture, developed over centuries and assumed to be part of the folk wisdom by which a group has survived. The needed changes to which bad cultural habits yield are slow and often indirect.

These clearly feminist notes, designed by and assumed to be for a male preacher, have no reason to be binding. Know that my gender concerns parallel my ethnic concerns; thus I have not accepted invitations to speak on civil rights in white churches. You see, I avoid the risk of seeming to plead for what is mine already. Regarding gender issues, I believe women should celebrate the good gospel rather than scold or argue an already well-documented case for rights.

The behavioral purpose of this strangely gripping Word must not be mistaken for a well-deserved diatribe on men. Its purpose is to move nameless missionary women to even higher service and still deeper rewarding joy. (Any result in improved male recognition is incidental.)

The moves in consciousness build to an enriching continuation of this tradition:

Move 1: Missionary Women began without recognition, but with the huge devotion needed for them to endure the hardships of their time and place.

Move 2: The Bible record tends to overlook their great and sacrificial support.

Move 3: Their labors were never in vain.

Move 4: We celebrate their significance and sure reward, with the Parable of the Last Judgment.

SERMON TEXT: LUKE 24:10
It was Mary Magdalene and Joanna, and Mary the mother of James, and other women that were with them, which told these things unto the apostles.

SERMON SUPPLEMENTARY TEXT: MARK 15:47
And Mary Magdalene and Mary the mother of Joses
beheld where he was laid.

Greatness: Named and Nameless

Happy Women's Day to all of you, my sisters and brothers in Christ! For those of you some call CME visitors, I pray that we can make the worship and the gospel so fresh and interesting that you will realize what you have been missing.

In order to get started, I invite you all to take out the pew Bible and turn to Luke 24:10. Let us all read together: "It was Mary Magdalene and Joanna, and Mary the mother of James, and other women that were with them, which told these things unto the apostles."

Now, place a marker there and turn to Mark 15:47. Let's read together again: "And Mary Magdalene and Mary the mother of Joses beheld where he was laid."

Now, let us refer to Luke 24:10. Join me in examining what is between the lines and out of sight.

This is one of the most important stories in the whole Bible. These women are the first to know of and announce the resurrection! The menfolk have given up already and gone back to fishing (John 21:3). Those women get credit for being anxious to bring some tenderness to this crushingly cruel situation.

I figure between the lines that these women were so devoted they did not get a wink of sleep. First, they had to find and wake up a sidewalk salesperson of burial spices to buy a sizeable supply of burial spices. Then they had to prepare the spices, after which they went on foot, in semi-darkness, back to the tomb. They arrived just before sun-up or daybreak. I figure that is almost five o'clock in the morning.

Now, I wonder why they saved only three names on the record Luke borrowed for his gospel record. It had to be that they gave the most money. First was Mary Magdalene, who was awesomely grateful for her healing from seven demons (Mark 16:9). She was generous in supporting Jesus' ministry.[1] She is the only woman not defined by a husband.

The second was Joanna, wife of Chuza, the head steward of the king's palace. She too was likely healed[2] and grateful and generous. She obviously received full permission from her busy husband to follow and support Jesus.

The third was Mary (or Salome), mother of James and Joses. She was not likely a financial supporter. Nevertheless, as mother of an apostle, she had a firm place among the women. She had a close tie with Jesus.

It is time, now, to look at "the other women that were with them," the ones who are nameless. Strange as it may seem, the Bible leaves hundreds of women nameless,[3] mothers included. There are few exceptions. Jochebed, Moses' mother, is mentioned in Exodus 6:20 and Numbers 26:59, and, of course, much mention is made of Mary, Jesus' mother. Jesus' genealogy in Matthew 1 includes two of Jesus' ancestral mothers, Rahab and Tamar—strange choice indeed. The rest of the names are male, followed by "begat," as if the ancestral fathers gave birth. You should note, the writers were not snubbing these other women at the tomb; they were just giving them equal injustice and gender discrimination.

I wonder how many saintly sisters feel treated the same way today. What can we learn from this namelessness?

First, through these women I can see a brave, huge, countercultural devotion to Jesus. We have no notion of how many they were, but we know they stuck close together as a group, to protect their reputations. This meant also that they gave more support and physical protection to Jesus as well as themselves. To stop this movement, the high priest and his soldiers had to pick a time when these other women, and men like them, were not around. That is why Jesus was arrested late at night.

A further measure of their devotion is evident when we think of their feet. These women followed Jesus on feet protected by flimsy sandals. After walking on rough and rocky roads, their feet were blisteringly hot, baked by the sun. When they were not walking, they were standing, since all of Jesus' gatherings were in the open air. These other women endured much just to walk where Jesus walked and to be near when he talked.

Then there were some people from far away. For instance, we know that Mary (Salome) came from up in Galilee with her sons. We know that they traveled by foot to Jerusalem, and it must be close to a hundred miles from Galilee to Jerusalem. How would we like to walk that far and then spend the days standing up in a crowd, listening to Jesus?

We do not know how many other mothers or fathers with children came from long distances. Nor do we have any notion what they ate or where they slept that far away from home. We can only be certain that every one of the other nameless women at the tomb was a great woman in her own right. They wanted just to be there—named and nameless.

I do not believe that Mary Magdalene, Joanna, Mary (Salome), or any of the unnamed sisters were concerned about greatness. When they stayed up all night and came early to the grave, the one thing on their minds was some last amenity for the human temple once occupied by Jesus of Nazareth. They adored him and sought to serve him without knowing that he was the Son of God and Savior.

I wish I knew more to tell you about those nameless other women. I can only confess that writing and preaching about them has taught me a lesson. You see, I think of those women as Jesus' first missionary society, forerunners of women's ministries today. While I have been critical of the Bible's omission of hundreds of women's names, the Spirit suddenly asked me the names of seriously serving women in churches of which I have been a member. Quite honestly, out of membership in eleven different congregations from coast to coast, in eighty-six years, I can remember the names of only two. They were presidents of women's ministries at two of the churches where I served as pastor.

This is not because I did not know or work with the others, serving as a regional director of local mission projects for fourteen years. Furthermore, I do not remember a women's leader ever denying assistance with a new project when help was offered. Most of the time, they were looking for meaningful labor.

As you can see, I am embarrassed that most of the women who helped me sixty years ago are still nameless. Although I may not remember their names, I cannot forget their great works. These women have labored to help establish an ultra-modern, fully furnished nursery at great sacrifice; offered love and kindness during a nonstop bedside vigil for a sister going home; and even hammered nails into siding on a Habitat for Humanity home. Just to see the joy in their faces from their commitment to God in serving others was a blessing.

Thankfully, for them and for me, this is not the last word in the matter. Jesus of Nazareth and Paul of Tarsus have encouraging words for the nameless and seemingly forgotten. After a masterful argument for eternal life, Paul says, "Therefore, my beloved brethren [*and sisters*], be ye stedfast, unmoveable, always abounding in the work of the Lord, forasmuch as ye know that your labour is not in vain in the Lord" (1 Corinthians 15:58).

The fact that you are overlooked and nameless is unimportant. That is not what we are working for in the first place. What counts is the fact that your blood, sweat, and tears are not useless or wasted. You may not see the results right away, or even in this life. The fact is that your efforts for the Lord are most assuredly useful in the kingdom. The most gratifying gratitude you will ever receive will be for things you did not know you did, at times of which you were not aware.

This reminds me of the parable of the last judgment that Jesus told to illustrate the second of our two concluding words: Not only is our labor never in vain, but also our labors in helping those who cannot help themselves will attain rewards beyond our fondest imagination.

In honor of those named and nameless women at the tomb, let us close with an updated paraphrase of the last judgment given to me.

PARABLE OF THE LAST JUDGMENT

Then shall the Chief Justice of the Supreme Court of heaven call an assembly of all the nations on planet Earth. He shall divide the people according to those who tried to follow the rules that came from heaven and those who did not. Just as a farmer might separate sheep from goats, or ducks from chickens, he will send the righteous citizens to his right hand side and the disobedient unrighteous to his left.

When all the papers are cleared and handed in, the Chief Justice will call the assembly to order. Then he shall turn to his right and declare officially, "You are hereby permitted and cordially invited to inherit a portion of space prepared for you from the beginning, when heaven was first founded. You have come to my aid in every state of hunger, nakedness, illness, jail, and homelessness." Then the righteous shall say, "Why us? When in the world did we ever see you hungry, thirsty, ragged, or homeless?" And the Chief Justice shall answer, "Let me assure you this is how we reward people who voluntarily feed and clothe the needy, visit the sick and shut-in, give hope to the incarcerated, offer a safe place for the homeless to sleep, or help find a job to restore the self-respect of the unemployed. Now, inasmuch as you did all these things for the neediest folks in the world, you did them for me."

Then the Chief Justice shall turn to those at his left and say, "Get out of my face, you greedy, cold-hearted unrighteous. There is a special place prepared for you, with the devil and his angels. Your space is for all eternity. Likewise, space for the righteous is for life eternal."

Thus briefly did Matthew end the record of the parable, but its powerful truth speaks on forever. It does not matter how long or short the written praise may be here on earth. The righteous in the parable had not kept score. They were too busy enjoying God's guidance and the abundant life in God's will.

Although the story was a parable, those other nameless women were real. The reward for their greatness is also real. The depth of joy and satisfaction in the very soul of sister veterans of suffering service is heard in the spiritual [singing out]: "I Wouldn't Take Nothing for My Journey."

Notes

1. Edith Deen, *All of the Women of the Bible* (New York: Harper & Brothers, 1955), 203.

2. Deen, 274.

3. Deen, xxi.

10

PASTOR'S ANNIVERSARY

IN SOME CULTURES, it is common to celebrate pastoral anniversaries each year. This guarantees that at least during one weekend per year, the congregation demonstrates its appreciation for the pastor's labors. Special offerings are given to the pastor as an expression of love and appreciation. This encouragement is often greatly needed, as well as deserved. However, there are churches where these anniversaries are the focus of the entire program year, even for the year's finances. This gift helps to compensate for the low regular salary, or for the lack of pension provisions, or both. These supplements to salary are not usually set aside for pension purposes, however—an error that is chargeable to pastor and people.

This writing can mention only briefly the obligation to correct this failure to provide for old age, when needed. Likewise, only brief mention can be made of the fact that now the Ministers and Missionaries Benefit Board (MMBB) is open to serving the pastors of non-member churches.

A second needed revision for this type of anniversary celebration is for focus on the quality of ministry. Frankly, the greatest honor one can give a pastor or a historic congregation is an increase in the effectiveness of its ministries rendered. This is assuming, of course, that salary and pension issues have been resolved. If not, then the congregation is obligated to take the initiative. This avoids the conversion of all anniversaries into thinly veiled begging or fundraisers. The giving of such special offerings needs to become true and responsible stewardship.

One working model was in practice in a congregation in California, with many members employed on a nearby military base. Every time these members received a raise in salary, the pastor's salary was increased by the same percentage. They freed their pastor to focus on empowering the congregation as a whole to be effectively ministering followers of Christ.

The sermon that follows is based on John 13, the familiar passage that records Jesus washing the disciples' feet. The non-traditional message from this text is about Peter's growth in response to Jesus' challenging example. The behavioral purpose is to move hearers to aspire to Jesus' example of humble service. The hearer is led to identify with Peter and to grow as Peter grew. (Emphasis is placed on the foot-washing incident.) The main vehicle of encounter is a character sketch. The moves are the stages of Peter's life. The final celebration praises Jesus and Peter for the Cathedral in Rome, and its worldwide congregation. The whole sermon openly implies parallel honor on the local pastor/servant.

Move 1: Peter enjoyed serving as spokesperson for the first disciples, as chosen by Jesus.

Move 2: Egotistic pride caused his denial of Jesus, and his self understanding led to repentance.

Move 3: Celebrate Peter as the main leader of the launch of the Church in "all the world."

SERMON TEXT: JOHN 13:15
For I have given you an example, that you should do as I have done to you.

SERMON SUPPLEMENTARY TEXT: ACTS 3:6
Then Peter said, Silver and gold have I none; but
such as I have I give thee: In the name of Jesus Christ
of Nazareth, rise up and walk.

Of Glory and Christian Service

I greet you in Jesus' joy, on the auspicious occasion of the
[insert pastor's anniversary year] anniversary of [insert pastor's name] as the honorable pastor of this great congregation. I deem it an honor to be invited, and I thank you most
sincerely. However, I beg your forbearance as I follow the
Spirit's guidance.

In the name of our nontraditional Lord and Savior, and
in honor of your unusually creative pastor, my friend, I invite your attention to an atypical anniversary lesson and text.
Please turn with me to the Gospel of John 13:1-17.

> Now before the feast of the Passover, when Jesus knew
> that his hour was come that he should depart out of
> this world unto the Father, having loved his own which
> were in the world, he loved them unto the end. And
> supper being ended, the devil having now put into the
> heart of Judas Iscariot, Simon's son, to betray him; Je-
> sus knowing that the Father had given all things into
> his hands, and that he was come from God, and went
> to God; He riseth from supper, and laid aside his gar-
> ments; and took a towel, and girded himself. After that
> he poureth water into a basin, and began to wash the
> disciples' feet, and to wipe them with the towel where-
> with he was girded. Then cometh he to Simon Peter:
> and Peter saith unto him, Lord, dost thou wash my
> feet? Jesus answered and said unto him, What I do thou
> knowest not now; but thou shalt know hereafter. Peter

saith unto him, Thou shalt never wash my feet. Jesus answered him, If I wash thee not, thou hast no part with me. Simon Peter saith unto him, Lord, not my feet only, but also my hands and my head. Jesus saith to him, He that is washed needeth not save to wash his feet, but is clean every whit: and ye are clean, but not all. For he knew who should betray him; therefore said he, Ye are not all clean. So after he had washed their feet, and had taken his garments, and was set down again, he said unto them, Know ye what I have done to you? Ye call me Master and Lord: and ye say well; for so I am. If I then, your Lord and Master, have washed your feet; ye also ought to wash one another's feet. For I have given you an example, that ye should do as I have done to you. Verily, verily, I say unto you, The servant is not greater than his lord; neither he that is sent greater than he that sent him. If ye know these things, happy are ye if ye do them.

"For I have given you an example, that ye should do as I have done to you."

Now, of course, you are wondering what Jesus' bathing of dusty feet has to do with an anniversary. I hasten to explain: Our focus is on Peter, a successful fishing foreman and the easily recognized spokesman and leader of the twelve disciples. I invite you to watch him closely, because he is typical of some of us. "He is we" is more proper to say, but "he is us" sounds better. He is us, in the sense that he is like some people we know, including ourselves. The similarity to us is in our attitudes toward the offices we hold. We need to see him before the crucifixion and then after Jesus departed and left him in the leadership of the movement.

The point at the outset was that Peter was relatively comfortable and happy to be who he was, as lead disciple. Then suddenly he was jarred, shocked, knocked for a loop. This Jesus who had given him an attractively high position—this

Jesus on whom he depended to keep this position—was down on the floor. Under his breath Peter was saying, "His towel is on his arm, and he is washing dirty feet, acting like a slave—a slave! What on earth is he thinking? He shall not wash *my* feet and get *me* involved in whatever this is that he is up to. I have worked too hard and long to get where I am. It's downright revolting to see my leader on his knees on the floor, caressing the dirty hooves of us disciples!"

Then he said aloud, "You'll not wash *my* feet, 'cause I think too much of you to cooperate in this put-down. I don't know who is responsible, or why, but count me out. You shall not wash *my* feet, while I rear back in haughty pride and play like you are my slave—no way, José!"

Jesus calmly replied, "Okay! Of course, if you are determined not to let me wash your feet, you cannot continue to have a part with me. You're either with me all the way, or you're not." Peter did not want to risk losing it all, so he leaped to the other extreme: "Well, then, don't just wash my feet. Wash my hands and my head also." Jesus assured him that disciples did not need all of that, but he almost casually dropped the hint that one of them would not be clean, as he continued to finish the feet of the rest of the disciples.

Jesus sat down then, and explained that he was giving them an example of how to minister—in living color. Then he really shocked them with the fact he was going to be betrayed. Peter was still a little unsure of how he stood with Jesus, so he asked John to ask Jesus who was the betrayer (John 13:24). Still overly conscious of position, Peter had not started to learn the profound meaning of the footbaths Jesus gave: humble service. Jesus had acted out a living example of humble service, and Peter was not even on the same page.

I am sure somebody is asking, "Why is this preacher so hard on Peter now? He did not sound so critical at first. Jesus did say he'd build his church on such a rock, didn't he?" Of course, he did! And he is still building his church on people whom he knows to be like Peter and many of us good disciples: we cherish high office above humble service, too. We too miss the point of Jesus' example. Let us take one final look at the lesser side of Peter and, maybe, incidentally, of us. Then we will get to the better part of Peter's living response to Jesus' example.

You see, we dare not miss Peter in the high priest's palace yard. Jesus was inside the hall, enduring a mock trial, and Peter was out there all alone, among strangers. As he stood with them by the fire, he couldn't handle not having his usual audience. So he started trying to chat himself up a crowd. It did not work. His countrified Galilean accent gave him away. When challenged by three different people, he did just what Jesus said he would: he denied Jesus three times! Just about that time he saw Jesus being led out by soldiers, and Jesus saw Peter—caught him with his mouth wide open, so to speak. Peter remembered what he had just promised and what Jesus had predicted, as the cock crowed. Peter went out and wept bitterly (Matthew 26:75). I mean big, bad fisherman Peter sneaked out of sight and cried like a baby.

I felt sorry for him, just reading about it, but I know now that it was good for him to cry, for he had been led to truly and deeply repent. Now Jesus' example of humble service could come to life in Peter's witness in ways that must have delighted Jesus later: to see the Peter he had prophesied, serving as the humble, hard-working rock on which the first churches were built.

When I started collecting Peter's unwritten record (the part in which Luke's book of Acts didn't see or know about), I had to begin to make assumptions about his itineraries. After Acts 12, Luke started emphasizing that brilliant missionary named Paul, when he came on the scene. I suppose there were much better written records available for him. Nevertheless, look at what we missed all these years, while popular secular fiction visualized Peter as the big, tough, profane leader of small fishing crews. Let us see how the Peter not found in Acts adopted Jesus' humble foot-washing example.

The first thing I see, after the repentance for the denials, is an amazingly powerful preacher. Luke covered him well (Acts 2). I can easily see the force of his personality. Where did he find the time to memorize all that Old Testament data he was putting down with no notes? He was not reading a manuscript. Where did he attain the oratorical skill and the handling of huge crowds? I am sure Jesus knew God had given him all of these gifts, but why haven't preachers and teachers mentioned Peter as they did Paul?

Then there must have been some recall of Jesus' teaching. Yet, there is very little in the record, and Peter preached these long, long sermons, from here to yonder in the Bible. In any case, Peter, the rough fisherman from Galilee, must have been greatly gifted with memory. His workload as preacher was only a part of his labor. There was no church, as we know it, and there was no organized congregation as such. Peter was the early chair of a board of apostles, period. So he did all the main leadership not recorded about the first few months and maybe years of what became the church. Yet he who once craved the top spot bore all that inescapable responsibility in low key, without bragging or complaining.

Can you imagine a leader of a movement that large being flat broke? Acts 3:6 casually declares that Peter and John, as they entered the temple, frankly admitted that they had no cash. They didn't even have anything to drop in the official offering plate. The healing they gave, nevertheless, was better than money and was a perfect copy of Jesus' humble example of care and healing.

In today's age of millionaire televangelists, it is not easy to imagine a media preacher with an audience of thousands having no money in his pockets. Penniless Peter deserves untold credit for his adherence to Jesus' example of humility, which was most certainly at heart of the foot bathing.

Peter promised Jesus that he would feed the sheep (John 21:15-17), and he surely did. Chapters 2 and 3 of the book of Acts are full of his preaching, feeding thousands the gospel.

Utterly unlike the original Peter, he took no bows, even though he was a powerful preacher.

One has to marvel at Peter's awesome authority. Acts 5:3 reports Peter questioning Ananias about the proceeds of a sale. Can you imagine a congregation in which members sell all they have and lay the proceeds at the feet of the pastoral staff to distribute to the needy? They still gathered in homes. They did not yet have the New Testament, but it is clear that the apostles fared well. However, Peter preached the gospel, as he promised.

Having served fourteen years organizing new congregations, Peter meekly accepted the decision of the board of apostles (there was no organized church yet) to send him out on the mission field. In most cases, audiences had not even heard of Jesus. I cannot even imagine how hard it must have been at the beginning. Yet Peter left the comfort of the big city and the evolving first church to go to and fro starting from zero. Most of the apostles stayed in the comfort of Jerusalem, preaching and teaching in existing synagogues and the temple. They had not been ordered by Jesus to withdraw from the traditional Hebrew congregations. It took a while to build centers for worship, not to mention growing as an organized body under the persecution that developed.

Yet Peter stayed busy, fruitfully. From a Jewish cult of Jesus followers, to the worldwide church of Jesus Christ, the early movement owes much to Peter. Expansion beyond Judaism came to Peter while on one of his preaching missions, to Joppa. The Spirit first gave Peter the vision that opened the way to Peter's acceptance of Gentiles. In humble obedience, Peter saw clearly that God is "no respecter of persons" (Acts 10:34). That is what Jesus intended by his Great Commission to "all nations" (Matthew 28:19).

Acts 10:34 was a monumental contribution, bringing radical change, and cited frequently even today in race relations. I cannot remember when I first learned to recite "no respecter of persons." Nevertheless, it had not come to Peter easily. In fact, Peter offered some resistance to change: "Not so, Lord; for I have never eaten any thing that is common or unclean" (Acts 10:14). It took three repetitions for Peter to yield, but this kind of final obedience to the guidance of the Spirit may be the most important aspect of Jesus' entire example. It connects with Jesus' example of ultimate submission to God's will in the Garden of Gethsemane: "O my Father, if it be possible, let this cup pass from me: nevertheless not as I will, but as thou wilt" (Matthew 26:39).

This all adds up to an amazing record, not gathered in major detail and carefully preserved anywhere in the Bible. I wondered how the Word could miss so much, and how the credit and glory could be so unequally and unjustly distributed. I confess that I had rather deep feelings of sympathy for Peter, as one often relates to what we call the underdog. I tend to feel like he had been mistreated, until I came to two interesting and healing insights.

The first was that Peter's options were severely limited. It was through no fault of his, and there was nobody else to blame. Unlike Paul, who was fully bilingual, Peter would have learned very little Greek while growing up in Galilee. Thus, he and Paul agreed to specialize with Paul serving the larger, richer Hellenistic congregations and Peter leading the more limited Aramaic-speaking believers. Peter was wise not to complain, accepting the facts of life. He wins my loyalty and support because he followed the graciousness and humility of his foot-bathing, humble Lord. He wasted no time wishing for the good old days when he was the unquestioned leader.

There is no sure way of knowing how Peter taught or preached to Cornelius, the Roman centurion (Acts 10:34-43). However, it is likely that this generous and effective army occupation officer and his family had learned the local dialect. Luke said Cornelius loved their nation, worshiped their God in his home, and built them a synagogue (Luke 7:5). Thus, even without any Greek, Peter may have been used to lead the first Gentile to Christ.

Peter could not read or write, and Silvanus (Silas) wrote his letters for him (1 Peter 5:12). Some of the things I once thought Peter deserved could not be given simply because he was not prepared to receive them. I cannot say how he managed to preach all the way to Rome in his later years. I am just glad he got there, able to complete in a most powerful way his last instance of following Jesus' awesome example.

We don't know what finally happened to most of Jesus' twelve disciples turned apostles, but we do know that Peter finally arrived at Rome. He was not there many years before he was crucified head down, as reported by Origen, a third-century church father.[1] We can only say that Jesus' example did not end with the crucifixion, and neither did Peter's. He had no visible resurrection, but his name is everywhere—less glorified only than that of Jesus. There is an ultimate justice here, visible even to this feeble intelligence.

It dawned on me one day as I stood for the first time in Rome, the center of the great Roman Catholic Church. Before me was this huge, awesome cathedral, the largest I had ever seen, in fact. It was the mother church to millions all over the world. People from every corner of the earth make pilgrimages to this place. Moreover, the name of this almost endless sanctuary is the Cathedral of St. Peter—Peter! The name lives on, and so does the example he learned to live by.

Glory to God in the highest!

Note

1. Floyd V. Filson, "Peter," *The Interpreter's Dictionary of the Bible*, 4 vols. (Nashville: Abingdon, 1962), 3:755.

11

Men's Day

HEARERS HAD GREAT interest, involvement, and understanding because Jesus used real-life metaphors (parables) to teach. One of his favorites centered on carpentry; he spoke of estimating construction costs and building on solid rock.

Likewise, the sermon that follows employs the craft of auto engine repair. Curious about the title, "Of Men and Motors," a diesel mechanic was lured into morning worship. He was later so blessed by the gospel in mechanical terms that he continued in dialogue with the pastor and his wife at dinner in their home, accompanied by his delighted companion. The Word comes alive, indeed, in the context where people live and work, more than forty hours per week.

The behavioral purpose of this sermon is to move men (and women) to be as careful and disciplined about their habits of hot temper as they are about their motor's habit of overheating. The setting is a narrative of a trip to a convention, but the substance is in moves built on three parts of every motor. The celebration is about our safe, cross-country arrival in a discarded car, rescued from a wrecking yard, with a rebuilt cooling system. The moves are:

Move 1: Motors need frequent checking for loose bolts and clamps that can cause leaks.

Move 2:   Motors need working thermostats that accurately read motor temperatures.

Move 3:   Motors need flushed radiators, free of clogging by rust, grease, and other foreign matter.

Move 4:   Celebrate junked cars that can be driven across the country with rebuilt cooling systems.

SERMON TEXT: GALATIANS 5:22
But the fruit of the Spirit is love, joy, peace, longsuffering, gentleness, goodness, faith . . .

Of Men and Motors

Ella and I were driving across from southern California to Miami, bound for a Baptist convention. At the same time, a well-used Plymouth two-door would soon arrive for our son in his second year in college in the same city. As I drove across the Arizona desert, in 110-degree heat, I noted a strange variety of cars parked on the side, each with its hood raised up.

I wondered to Ella what might be the common cause of their problem. It was not that they were all small cars; there were large cars also. There were not just old cars that stalled; there were a few flashy new ones as well. It could not have been that they were overloaded; there were more one-passenger pick-ups and sedans than fully packed cars, by far. Nobody dared to claim climbing high mountains; that desert was flat as a pancake for miles.

Suddenly, an exciting idea came to me. I asked Ella to get a pen and paper, and she began to record a rough draft of a sermon for me.

The problem in common among all those cars was an inadequate cooling system. This condition was just as true among a few hot-tempered saints in churches where I had labored. It was not like cars, where older ones get hotter. The church's younger saints tended to get hot quicker. Otherwise, they were all about the same. The more I saw hot motors, the more I could see similarities in hot, angry people. Stirring in my mind were three general types of problems and care: carelessness versus discipline, paranoid misjudgment, and the pollution of selfishness.

First, every automobile owner needs the weekly, even daily discipline of engine check-ups. So many things can come loose: fan belts, hose clamps, bolts on motor head gaskets and crankcases. Just because one's engine keeps running after a few oil drops on the floor does not mean it is safe to continue driving without a check-up or repair. Too many folks postpone repairing a car, until one day, many miles from home, the car overheats and the engine block is ruined. You now have to replace it at a humongous expense! Now you can no longer afford to drive.

Cars cared for routinely and systematically can run for more than two hundred thousand miles. People need the same kind of check-ups, physically and spiritually. A disciplined review of daily or yearly plans could help avoid many simple errors or wastes. Adhering to a good diet and eliminating poor eating habits and foods, combined with a course of exercise, could work wonders on many who for now prefer just to let the oil drop, so to speak. Reaching ninety-plus years is my testimony for proper diets, swims, and annual check-ups.

Spiritual check-ups in the form of morning prayer are remarkably blessed. A hard-working, sincere brother of sixty-one had never done more than a routine morning prayer. After suffering a mild heart attack, he became acutely aware that it was a clear signal that he needed the calming of his spirit. He had been too uptight and impatient. He started meditative prayer first thing every morning, and he enjoys life now, as he had never before known how. His spiritual motor idles well and bursts with power when needed.

The second type of problem and care I call paranoid mis-judgment. It runs parallel to the function of the thermostat for a motor—to control the cooling system. If the motor is too hot, it triggers the cooling system to cool the motor down and get it out of danger. If the motor is slow warming up, it helps stop the flow of coolant until the motor is warm enough to function well.

The problem occurs when the thermostat malfunctions and misreads the temperature. If it thinks the motor is too cold and triggers too much heat, it causes the motor to over-heat. If it thinks the motor is too hot and causes the motor to overcool, it hampers lubrication. The usual remedy is a new thermostat. Most people do not perform this type of repair themselves. It is too complicated.

There are a number of Christians with bad thermostats. They read friends as enemies and have trouble trusting and loving folks. They perceive the community's climate to be cold, and they turn up the heat of anger and suspicion and defensiveness. They need the cure of becoming radically new persons in Jesus Christ.

Jesus himself became the victim of false witnesses (Luke 23:2). He had every reason to be angry and impatient with church leaders who flatly lied about him, saying he opposed paying Roman taxes. Yet, Jesus maintained his cool. Do you see what I mean? We need new persons in Christ, people with Christ-like spiritual thermostats, who help all of us to keep cool regardless.

The third area of motor care was much more common when I was a boy, in the 1920s. It had to do with foreign materials in the radiator, such as dirt or trash. I was not old enough to know how that stuff got in there, but I knew it had to come out. Even a nine-year-old could open the cap and clean the screen. One frequently sees adults draining the cooling system and refilling it with fresh water and antifreeze. It simply has to be done!

The most common dirt in today's spiritual cooling systems I call "self." Just as trash clogs the flow of the coolant
and makes the motor run hot, so self-centeredness chokes the
flow of human love and understanding and forgiveness. It
makes good Christians run hot. It is amazing how suddenly
some people reveal themselves as impatient and impossibly
self-centered and proud—folks we had long thought of as
Christ-like.

I think, for instance, of Euodias and Syntyche, strong
leaders in the church at Philippi (Philippians 4:2). There was
a conflict of opinion going on between them, pride verses
pride. These dear sisters stopped speaking to each other. The
apostle Paul begged his friends to help overcome their feeling
of mutual attack. He sought to grow a Christ-like spiritual
thermostat that would keep them warmly and lovingly engaged, not hotly hostile. His specifications for the thermostat
are found in Philippians 4:8: Engage in the discipline of concentrating on "whatsoever things are true, whatsoever things
are honest, whatsoever things are just, whatsoever things are
pure, whatsoever things are lovely, whatsoever things are
of good report; if there be any virtue, and if there be any
praise, think on these things." What a marvelous practical
recommendation!

What Paul requested remains badly needed today in congregations and in communities. If only this were as easy as
replacing a thermostat in your car. Of course, it is not. Nor is
it impossible. You just have to get started! Unfortunately, the
death of one resolves fierce oppositions too often, with the
sincere, although belated, regret of the other.

I have vivid recollections of steaming motors followed
by draining radiators, followed by a refill with clean water
and perhaps some antifreeze. Overheating was due to foreign
matter, such as trash clogging the flow. I do not recall the
cause, but the cure was simple: drain it out and fill it up with
clean water.

The thermostat is a complicated motor part which functions to avoid misreading the state of affairs. Its spiritual counterpart includes that somewhat complicated list that Paul suggested. The person who is like a dirty radiator is much simpler to correct. You just have to stop infantile assumptions that the whole world centers on you. It is an attitude that starts in spoiled brats and continues in some people throughout life. Some parents like to help you keep clogged up, dependent, or spoiled.

Every shade-tree mechanic knows that when there is dirt in a radiator, or a cooler hose, or a fuel line, there is nothing to do but clean it out. There are no shortcuts, unless you wish to destroy the engine. For these fifty-year-old self-clogged and spoiled husbands and wives, the simple solution is to grow up and take care of yourself and others. That goes for everybody, both older and younger. Do not wait until your parents are dying to try to clean the self out of your lines.

It does not take a rocket scientist to figure out how to grow up. All you have to do is try being healthily self-sufficient and then helping other people in addition. For example, thousands of people whose lives have been restricted to "gimme" have suddenly discovered a new joy as they have sacrificed to help flood victims. A newly cleaned and repaired radiator freely (and joyfully) performs its role of warming and cooling the car. So too, is every once-clogged soul bound to find joy in a Habitat for Humanity house, or the delivery of needed food or clothing, or any one of hundreds of church ministries of outreach. The writer of the book of James was right on target when he advised us to "count it all joy" (James 1:2).

The sum total influence of our parable of the motor is parallel to the influence of the parable of our text, which uses trees as its figure: "But the fruit of the Spirit is love, joy, peace, longsuffering, gentleness, goodness, faith," and so on. So also is the fruit of the labors of a worthy auto mechanic a quiet, peaceful, powerful, patient engine. What Jesus saw in carpentry, shepherding, and crops on trees, we today can parallel in the labor of auto mechanics.

Let us return to the spot where this sermon was first inspired and written down, during a ride through Arizona. First, let me confess that our mechanic selected our car from his junkyard. He told us that he was sorry he had not had time to road test it fully. However, he had carefully overhauled the cooling system, and he thought we could make it. We made it all the way to Florida from California without having to stop one time to open up our hood. Our son got his car, and it was so inexpensive it did not jeopardize his scholarship. Nor did it cause problems for us, especially since I was still recovering from heart trouble and was unemployed. That mechanic's care was a blessing unspeakable.

The moral to this story is clear: the motor in a well-maintained car will not get hot, break down, or blow up. When one is habitually careful with good maintenance, even a car nearly ten years old with high mileage will stand the wear and tear and pressure of a drive from coast to coast. But a nearly new car will fail if one has neglected to check everything. Human beings make cars, and they all break down.

The metaphors here are somewhat mixed, as the text says the power to be longsuffering comes from the Spirit. I surely believe it was the Spirit working in this parable. The Spirit guided the choice of the car by the mechanic. The Spirit guided the labor of the mechanic, both as to his skill and in his awesome generosity. The Spirit kept us safe and timely all the way. It was amazing grace.

However, the parallels between the overheated motor and the overheated human personality still hold. Every person familiar with automotive engine care is blessed by the ways a motor manual helps one to remember the disciplines of the care of the spirit. Today, we have focused especially on angry impatience and hot temper. We conclude with the true story of Harry, a great deacon, married to Mary, a great deaconess in a great church.

At dinner one day, Mary confided to me that her husband had not always been so smiling and gracious. There was a time early in their marriage when Harry's countenance would suddenly change, and he would have to leave the room to cover up his explosive temper. The veins in his temples would seem ready to pop, and yet nobody else would have a clue as to what had gotten into him.

Mary went on to say that Harry's mother had advised her not to take it too seriously. "He gits over it soon enough and he don't mean no harm." She said he had been that way all his life. It was as if he was born that way. "Why he used to git outrageous mad just a-settin' in the baby buggy."

Mary sighed, "Thank God, he got over it. And he's glad about it too." Seems he went to the doctor one day, and the doctor scared him half to death. He offered Harry the possibility of a stroke, and that was enough to convince him that there had to be a cure. When he asked his doctor about it, his reply was disarmingly simple: "I could send you to a professional psychologist, and he could help you. However, you would have to do most of the work. Why don't you try it on your own first? I happen to believe that serious prayer can help."

Mary thought it was risky when Harry told her, but the doctor tipped her off to his system of early warning and eased her concern. He set Harry to writing down when and why he had each attack. Harry began to tighten each loose bolt, as it were. The more he looked at each outbreak and prayed about it, the more he wondered why he ever let it happen in the first place. He had far less trouble than he expected tightening it up.

The doctor used Paul's prescription about thinking on these things, but Harry first thought about the things going wrong. Harry soon began to see and feel the difference. Mary could not point to an exact time, nor could Harry. Nevertheless, Harry was all but perfectly healed five years later. When I first met him five years after that, he was the most wonderful deacon I ever met. He reported as many as thirty house calls per month, visiting the sick, the shut-in, the church school absentees, and the bedside Baptists who picked up the newspaper and crawled back into bed. Harry became friends with all of them. Even when some did not appreciate the follow-up visits, we could trust Harry to be pleasant about it and make friends for the Lord and for his church.

We have used the motor trade to help us understand and work with our hot tempers. Where Jesus used a seamstress and patches for a parable on rips in relations, we can now add auto mechanics and computer geeks to the kingdom's crew of artisans. They all have ready access to the same spiritual tools that Harry had. Moreover, I declare unto you that God trusts and uses every single talent and trade that God ever gave anybody to keep the spiritual motors running cool and smoothly. This is yet another way of saying, with Paul, that the Spirit tree produces patience and longsuffering.

Glory hallelujah!

12

INDEPENDENCE DAY

WHO WOULD DARE deny that Independence Day is a great and meaningful national celebration? Yet, more often than not, we overlook the core of our country's Declaration of Independence: "We hold these truths to be self-evident, that all men are created equal, and that they are endowed by their Creator with certain inalienable rights."[1] Independence was the clearly expressed objective of our country's declaration. Yet the voice of the Creator who made the people and decreed that independent equality was soon silenced. That is, except when it became necessary to use the divine name to bolster unequal but superior rights and privilege for owners of land.

This oversight is all the more strange when we contemplate how far the ideas of freedom and equality had come in the Anglo-Saxon world from 1066 to 1776, the date of the declaration. The serfs of medieval Britain had been little different from African American slaves in status and function. Medieval serfs, however, had belonged with the land. These pilgrims, now long delivered from bondage to the land, had sought religious liberty. Meanwhile they had been part of an evolving white middle class. This, too, was considered as the will of God. Presumably, God wished to provide every English pioneer with ownership of some of the indigenous people's land.

Thus, any true celebration of independence must surely reconsider the place of the will of the acknowledged Creator, in secular policy as well as celebration. The behavioral purpose of the sermon should be to move patriots and the whole nation to be less content with inequality and injustice and to move closer to the righteous will of God. The life of the apostle Paul serves as a model for the needed move from smug contentment with the status quo to the will of God. His biography describes the process of growth, and the sermon text models the attitudinal goal or behavioral purpose.

The description of Saul's first step toward the new Paul is, by parallel identification, where many Americans start today. Thus, following the bridge-building introduction, we note the following moves in consciousness:

Move 1:   The early life of Saul, self-righteous Pharisee and zealous persecutor of the new church, provides a parallel with self-righteous Christians today.

Move 2:   The full experience of transition from Saul to Paul becomes an illustration of how we may also be transformed in the image of the risen Christ.

SERMON TEXT: PHILIPPIANS 3:11-14
If by any means I might attain unto the resurrection of the dead. Not as though I had already attained, either were already perfect: but I follow after, if that I may apprehend that for which also I am apprehended of Christ Jesus. Brethren, I count not myself to have apprehended: but this one thing I do, forgetting those things which are behind, and reaching forth unto those things which are before, I press toward the mark for the prize of the high calling of God in Christ Jesus.

Patriots in Christ

Hear ye! Hear ye!

"We hold these truths to be self-evident, that all men are created equal, and that they are endowed by their Creator with certain inalienable rights."[2] Did you hear that? These were words of the founding fathers of this country when they broke away from Great Britain. It is the second sentence of the Declaration of Independence. Our country was assuredly founded on a stated belief in God and God's rule of justice and righteousness.

Appropriate celebration of our independence needs not only to recognize the Creator in the wording of the declaration; God belongs significantly in every bit of traditional festivities celebrating the declared independence of our beautiful, spacious skies. How did the work and presence of God become secondary to food, fireworks, and other presumably patriotic expressions? That is if, indeed, God has ever been a serious influence in any of our typically patriotic events.

The greatest praise we can give the Creator, in addition to sincere worship, is to put forth a strenuous effort to make the United States a far better model of the practice of the just and righteous will of God. A good, healthy place to begin a Christian celebration of Independence Day is with the humble confession of the apostle Paul. He says, "I count not myself to have apprehended: but this one thing I do, forgetting those things which are behind, and reaching forth unto those things which are before, I press toward the mark for the prize of the high calling of God in Christ Jesus" (Philippians 3:13-14). In other words, it would be an interesting and appropriate action during our Independence Day worship to consider Paul's progress through life, from his excesses as a traditional Pharisee patriot to his awesome contribution to the Christian faith and the betterment of humankind.

Then, let us look at the pre-Damascus-Road Saul. He was a prototypical zealot, overly content with and conforming to customs as they were. His identification with the prevailing social system was too complete. In his early years in metropolitan Tarsus, he was compensating for his identity in the tiny minority of Jews. In Jerusalem, where he went for his Ivy League-level of legal training during his later years, he was a lesser Jew born in Tarsus. Saul was painfully sensitive to his lack of acceptance in either setting during his formative years.

His parents must have been fairly well off to send him away to school under Gamaliel. He used, however, this great scholar more as a credential than a mentor. While Professor Gamaliel could have been what we call a Hillel liberal today, Saul remained firmly fixed as a status-quo archconservative. Saul felt more secure hanging with the power and finance brokers of the ecclesiastical establishment. Moreover, they were in league with the Roman government and its military arm. He loved being in with the money and the might. It was a way to overcompensate for any shortfall in his status otherwise.

It is odd that Paul never mentioned how his parents pleased Rome and became Roman citizens. Their acceptance must have been a social liability inside his primary Jewish identity as a Hebrew of the Hebrews. His Roman credential was handy in places like Agrippa's court, and, of course, when working among the Gentiles in later years. The main point is that Saul enjoyed being a Roman for the sake of status. Nevertheless, he was never at peace—always trying to be something he feared he was not.

Among the extremes to which he went to please the bigwigs was his assent to the stoning of Stephen. That lynch crowd laid their clothing at the feet of this young man named Saul (Acts 7:58). It is easy to understand how he later spoke of his previous sinfulness in general terms and never dared share the grim, bloody reality of his prominent place in Stephen's death. I can't help believing that it was this scene which cracked Saul's crust of conformity to the establishment. Reaching into depths of his soul, the scene later transformed him on Damascus Road.

The case history of the United States as a nation is strikingly parallel to Paul's case. When our Euro-American leaders declared independence and then wrote the Constitution (1787), we were still at Paul's Pharisee stage of feeling threatened by people of differing faith and practice, and thus persecuting them. In fact, the Pilgrims had hardly settled in Plymouth in 1620, seeking freedom of religion, before Roger Williams received the order to leave the Colony of Massachusetts (1636) for thinking and speaking outside the customary beliefs of the colony. Religious freedoms were restricted as early as 140 years before the Declaration of Independence.

Parallel to Saul's subtle inferiority complex was the colony complex, evident well into the twentieth century. "We're as great as Great Britain. Hooray!" The marching bands and waving flags are a bit excessive among some even now. In the earlier years, their patriotic zeal was bordering on ridiculous. This is especially true in the light of data such as chattel slavery, witch hunts and executions, unpunished lynchings, and the fact that women weren't allowed to vote until 1922, three years after I was born.

When our Euro-American ancestors wrote slavery into law, they were doggedly determined to maintain the system of privilege that they enjoyed. Like Saul, the Pilgrims were utterly blind to any good idea or action that challenged their established beliefs and advantages. Therefore, the writers of the Constitution were retaining the same kinds of advantages as those from which their forebears had fled in the *Mayflower*. Thus, the freedom and independence designed by the pioneers contained flaws from the beginning.

In 1831, Samuel Francis Smith wrote the lyrics to "My Country, 'Tis of Thee." Unfortunately, the independence, freedom, and equality for all, along with the praise and thanksgiving to "Our fathers' God to thee, Author of liberty"[3] became lost in reality. Perhaps he should have rewritten the hymn to sing, "From every mountainside let freedom ring *for me and mine*."

When people sing "God Bless America," they seek special treatment for their special segment of America. If one wants to engage in sanctified self-centeredness, unashamed, the best place to do it is as a patriot. In addition, all the unjust advantages in either the early Saul or the early United States are backed up and enforced by money and military might, not by the Creator cited in the declaration. However, thank God, the story of Saul turned Paul does not end here, nor does the story of the United States.

The life story of Paul, as we have traced it so far, has given no hints of a positive ending. The anticipation of good news, however, has kept us watching. We already know where Paul's life is going. We just wonder how in the world such a bloodthirsty zealot could have become such a self-sacrificing major pillar of the Christian church. Likewise, we wonder how some of the major forces of banking and the military could have been so won over to equality, justice, and emergency aid as they are today.

We can see in retrospect what may have been Saul's first step toward the new Paul. He did a reevaluation of his treasured access to and influence with the temple and the money and military might of the Roman government. Philippians 3:7 states, "But what things were gain to me, those I counted loss for Christ."

As is always the case, there comes a time when we get disillusioned with the very things for which we once overcompensated. They looked impressive, but they didn't satisfy. While Saul seemed delighted with his power of life and death over those followers of Christ, the hole in his own soul was still there. Blood wasn't what the real Saul cried out for. God did not make him for animal-level relationships, and down deep, his own soul said so.

Saul never had been the devil he seemed to be at first glance. He was just becoming intimidated, and he overcompensated. He was typical of strivers who resort to extremes because they do not know of any better way to gain the up-front status they think they will enjoy. As Saul watched Stephen's blood flowing into the street and heard him pray for his murderers, he felt something rebel in his soul, and he was never the same after that. He sensed that he was going to have to face his Lord, and he had pushed it back as long as he could. The longer he delayed, the worse it became. We have to suspect that he had earlier premonitions. Notice how obedient he sounded immediately after finally being knocked down on the Damascus Road: "Lord, what wilt thou have me to do?" (Acts 9:6).

You should note that because Saul did not consider himself an intentional sinner in the first place, he did not convert. He thought of himself as pleasing God with his persecutions of Jesus' followers. In all his cruelty, Saul had meant well—he was following his self-centered misreading of the divine will. It was not until he witnessed the shocking, shattering suffering of saintly Stephen that he became prepared to hear and respond to the voice of God. It took a rare and awesome signal; then his change was complete.

So it is with many people today. They too mean well. They like to think that their rents, prices, and profits are within the will of God and the best of the American tradition of freedom. Foreclosures and firings are about as acceptable as the stoning of Stephen to those who are about as privileged as Saul and care little beyond their own. It takes startling messages from God, as rare as the shed blood of Stephen, to get the attention of the comfortable blest of our day who still do not care beyond their own class and nominal faith. That, too, is changing. This is not the end of the story in the United States. We have had a shocking message or two, and with parallel results.

I just read a report in the local newspaper that warmed my heart. A businessman, himself a recent amputee, went to Haiti after the earthquake and saw the virtually innumerable people injured and in need of limbs. He teamed up with a surgeon and a limb company, and they have already fitted two hundred Haitians, and they plan to continue. His report summed it up thus: "It's been absolutely life-changing. I have a new respect for the Haitian people, people I knew nothing about before. I have a renewed respect and love for God, seeing Him in these miracles."[4] Hundreds, if not thousands, heard and responded to this startling message from God.

The good news parallel to the apostle Paul's response to God's startling message is already well on its way in the United States!

The conclusion to Paul's story breaks away from the patriotic celebration: it is not what we might call a national brag—a glorification of "My country 'tis of thee . . . land of liberty." Paul (the new Saul by the time of this writing) said that, with all his later accomplishments, he had no notion that he had superior achievement. He was "forgetting those things which [were] behind [both good and evil], and reaching forth unto those things which are before," he was pressing "toward the mark for the prize of the high calling of God in Christ Jesus" (Philippians 3:13-14).

The ruthless striver who directed the stoning of no less a saint than Stephen ended his earthly career with untold churches and saved individuals to his credit, plus more writing credits than all the rest of the authors in the New Testament. He provided the best theological thinking of the early church, but his final concern was to keep pressing forward, not to the status of a leader of the temple establishment but to the mark set by his crucified Lord.

The parallel flow which we have been following between Paul and the United States provides little comparison with Paul's final score card, but there is some parallel news. The most effective recent comparables with the Damascus Road signal that shocked and prepared Saul/Paul to accept his calling have been Hurricane Katrina and the Haitian earthquake. As just reported, these have moved once-nominal Christians into sacrificial assistance toward the Jesus mark and beyond all previous expectation. In the Haitian earthquake, the cash and personal service responses have been awesome. Whole churches and communities who had never before given at all have dug deep and found joy. Busloads of church members have brought their tools and stayed a week. They report that while they have never seen such need, they have also never had such deep inner joy. This is patriotic service to our United States at its very highest and best.

Some of the most heroic service in our time has been from military personnel, and atypical of the earlier patriotic objectives of glorious warfare. I just read of a desperately needed school for girls in an isolated spot in Afghanistan, built by military personnel with their personal sacrifices of money. It also required their spare time. This kind of waging peace turns out to be more effective by far than the waging of violent warfare. Many soldiers would prefer this kind of the waging of peace as patriotic. I close with a story in that vein for our Independence Day patriotic worship celebration. I wrote it for telling at a U.S. Army chapel, for a Martin Luther King Jr. Day service.

As we drove down a two-lane road in South Carolina on a Sunday morning, five-year-old Korean Kim sat in back, watching everything. When we finally managed to pass the last unit of a long, slow military convoy, Kim protested profusely. He wanted me to stay close to the lead Jeep. On my third attempt to stretch on out, I asked, "Kimmie, how's come you don't want me to leave that Jeep?" He answered, "I like that man!" Well, the man looked all of seventeen, so I was sure Kim had not known him over in Korea. I wanted to know, "Why do you like that man?" To which Kim looked at me in scorn, implying, "You mean to tell me you didn't know that? Soldiers that drive Jeeps give candies and gum to little children." For the chapel, I added, "Soldiers who drive ambulances make dollies for little girls, and soldiers who drive trucks give hand-made toys to little boys."

It was plain that Kim considered a soldier's primary purpose to be that of kindness to little children. And it was clear that the soldiers had a heart for helping. They enjoyed waging peace with everything they had at their discretion. As I happened to look to my left, I saw the post commander, a major general. It was plain that he, too, would have gladly made peace his primary preference for pressing forward. He was so deeply moved by little Kim's opinion of soldiers that his face was bathed in tears.

Would to God that we might celebrate our independence by our pressing toward the prize of the calling of the Prince of peace!

Amen.

Notes

1. Second Continental Congress (September 5, 1775, to March 2, 1789), Declaration of Independence, July 4, 1776, www.archives.gov/exhibits/charters/declaration_transcript.html (accessed April 3, 2012).

2. Second Continental Congress, Declaration of Independence.

3. "My Country, 'Tis of Thee," en.wikipedia.org/w/index.php?title=My_Country,_%27Tis_of_Thee&oldid=455090110 (accessed October 11, 2011).

4. Bill Sanders, "Doctor, Amputee Help Earthquake Victims," *The Atlanta Journal-Constitution*, May 16, 2010, B3.

13

LABOR DAY

LABOR DAY WEEKEND is a good time for Christians to begin thinking about labor, employment, and earning a living in the terms of their faith. For most of us, a job or position takes up the largest block of time in our conscious day. Whatever kind of work we do, all of it is by the grace of God. Therefore, our attitude toward our work is likely to be our attitude toward life and toward God. The behavioral purpose of this sermon, then, is to move hearers to affirm and enjoy their jobs as gifts from God, not just a means to a paycheck.

The first national holiday honoring workers was in 1894. It celebrated belated deliverance from atrocious practices like twelve-hour days and seven-day workweeks, with child laborers as young as six years old. The path leading to these improvements was violent and bloody. It reflected the trauma of learning how to move from an agrarian economy into the Industrial Revolution.

The offspring of ex-slaves faced still another approach. The white benefactors of the newly established mission schools required that all college graduates be equipped with a manual trade. It was supposedly a resource in reserve. The unspoken theory was that they would not succeed in the professions and would need something to fall back on.

It is interesting to note that although the Old Testament celebrates work with hands, the New Testament, under Greek influence, exalts intellectual effort. Nevertheless, Jesus, son of a skilled carpenter, uses figures from carpentry when he talks of building cost estimates and foundations built on rock, not sand. The apostle Paul turns out to be, like Jesus, competent in both manual and intellectual labor. However, he is more of an outspoken advocate for manual labor, possibly compensating for the Greek imbalance. For the purposes of this weekend, Paul the writer-scholar and skilled tentmaker is a wonderfully relevant labor model, as well as being the assumed author of the sermon text.

First Thessalonians 4:11-12 is a brief, tightly packed set of insights on survival and witnessing in a pagan-majority society that was hostile to Christians. There were also some problems with aggressive Gnostic extremists. Such a spread in a problematic context is not unlike that which faithful Christians face today. Our emphasis on labor is compatible with Paul's main concern to keep the peace. The sermon is expository, using Paul's suggested characteristics as sermon moves in consciousness (points made to come alive).

Move 1:   Introduces both the church of Thessalonica and the apostle Paul in some detail.

Move 2:   Establishes the value of working with your own hands.

Move 3:   Offers advice on minding your business and the integrity of that work.

Move 4:   Closes with a celebration of the joy and satisfaction of manual labor, which is treated almost as a sacrament.

SERMON TEXT: 1 THESSALONIANS 4:11-12
And that ye study to be quiet, and to do your own business, and to work with your own hands, as we commanded you; that ye may walk honestly toward

them that are without, and that ye may have lack of
nothing.

The Sacrament of Labor

Happy Labor Day weekend! Welcome to the house of the
Lord, where we offer constant praise to our gracious God
and deal with the issues of the real world. Our issue this
morning is, of course, labor—work, jobs, tasks, and crafts.
This is a topic of great importance, and we should meditate
on it and pray about our own part in it much more often than
we probably do. I realize that we do pray constantly about
God's part in keeping us employed.

As we seek, for our worship, a word on labor from the
Word on all things, we turn to 1 Thessalonians 4:11-12.
That's page [mention page number] in your pew Bible. I in-
vite you to keep your Bible open throughout the sermon.

[Read aloud, beginning at 1 Thessalonians 4:9 to provide
a lead-in, and note the text at verse 11.]: "But as touching
brotherly love ye need not that I write unto you: for ye yourselves are taught of God to love one another. And indeed ye
do it toward all the brethren which are in all Macedonia: but
we beseech you, brethren, that ye increase more and more;
and that ye study to be quiet, and to do your own business,
and to work with your own hands, as we commanded you;
that ye may walk honestly toward them that are without, and
that ye may have lack of nothing."

To understand what was on Paul's mind, let us start with
the town, followed by the church and its needs. Thessalonica
was a busy port city of Macedonia, the country just north of
Greece. The people spoke the Greek language and worshiped
Greek gods. There were many non-Greeks, including enough
Jews to have a synagogue. This was Paul's base of opera-
tions, and the first converts were Gentiles whom Paul and his

company met "at church" in the synagogue. The Jews were hospitable but did not become converts to Christ.

The main preaching occurred in the streets, with most of the harvest gathered in the streets. This aroused the pagan majority, who drove Paul's missionary team out of town. This was after they had had only three weeks or so to get the church started. The letter was to new Christians, with not much teaching and under persecution after the apostles left. Therefore, Paul's letter had to deal with the basic issues of survival.

Thus, Paul's first word about being quiet was not because the Thessalonians had been rowdy. It was to be sure to attract as little attention as possible. This seems odd for a street preacher, of all people, to be advising somebody to keep quiet, but we must admit that it was wise. These inexperienced witnesses would hardly have known how to handle hostile mobs and prejudiced police. The civil rights demonstrators of our day had professional leaders and plenty of time to teach the hard disciplines needed for this type of risky demonstration. Never start any confrontational battles that you know you cannot win.

Paul's advice sounds like the advice we've heard all our lives: "Mind your own business!" Nosy folks can get into a lot of trouble. You may need to know many things to be able to help a sinner. However, please do not sound like a prosecuting attorney, engaged in cross-examination. Let them tell you what they want you to know.

Paul's next item of advice raises the issue of greatest interest to us today: "work with your own hands." In our world of automatic everything, this must not be mistaken for a promotion from a labor union. Rather, in Paul's mind, it was almost all there was for jobs, except for drivers and haulers and the army. Almost everything else was done with their hands. With all this practical usefulness, hands also took on symbolic usages. Creation itself was from the hands of God, along with much of God's current works with and for humankind. We still have no better expressive words for the purpose than "the hand of God."

The image of the creativity of all work with hands became dim by the time of slavery and its cruel compulsion. Yet, the beauty of slave labor in wrought iron and great mansions was recognized notwithstanding. Slaves themselves realized that labor was inherently precious, even though they looked forward to rocking chairs in heaven. Once they were free, their work with their hands changed from sentence to sacrament. Indeed, one gets the impression that work was a kind of sacrament in the life of tentmaker Paul, also.

Paul wanted to be sure that these new Christians were above reproach in the labor they offered and the things they sold. He wanted them "that are without" to choose these Christians within as better than, so that they would seek them out again, regardless of their strange faith. This would mean that these saints should have a reputation for honesty and excellence. I suspect Paul believed, as I do, that good artisans tend to be dependable for high quality. People trust them. They know that good workmanship leaves no need to cheat. Just pay what they ask, and gladly.

So many people in business today take shortcuts and bend rules. When we find business people we know we can trust, we enjoy time spent in their presence. I enjoy, for example, stopping at my auto repair shop, even though the repairs I need are costly. The same is true of the woman who prepares my manuscripts for the press. It is just good to know that they know, and that they are nice and not arrogant about it. This level of labor and attitude is what we celebrate.

If you still have your Bibles open, look at the closing clause of verse 13: "that you may have lack of nothing." Please notice, in this concentrated packet of wisdom, the last advice about working in hostile Thessalonica is about paychecks, earned so you will not need anything. In other words, you go to work because you and your family need to eat regularly.

This, however, is Paul's least important reason for labor. He is quite right. Do not go to work with an attitude of dire necessity and desperation. It is much easier and more pleasant to go gladly to work, happy to be where God made it possible and doing what God called you to do.

As for our hands, power tools and computers have replaced them in home and industry. Many of us are compelled to improvise uses for our hands, for the good of our hands and for the holistic fulfilling of our entire being.

One of the most gifted people I know is an expert worker on computers, but he uses his hands quite a bit. He does his hardest work in his head, of course. Yet his hands are fulfilled—busy and productive. He uses meters and screwdrivers. Thank the Lord!

Most of us are not able to use our hands on our computers. We need to carve wood, or sew leather, like Paul and Priscilla, or become gourmet cooks if we plan to keep on eating. We need a combination—some creative use that keeps hands active so they will not atrophy.

The contract auditor for our office had an enviable combination. He played an organ concert on the air every morning. I, along with thousands of others, was blessed to hear him. Then he left the studio and went to his accounting work. On his way home, he played another relaxed, effortless concert from his huge, memorized repertoire of timeless organ masterpieces. That was the abundant life Jesus came to bring, if ever I saw one!

Too many impressions about labor are negative, depicting work as undesirable. We need to clear the air and speak to the ultimate standing of labor in the kingdom of God. For instance, it is important for children to understand that none of the necessary work in a happy home is undesirable. This means that parents have to avoid giving the possible impression that children wash dishes simply because they are powerless. Too often, this assignment becomes a test of parental authority and power and a means of teaching children to be responsible. It becomes a means of parents avoiding the task they themselves hate, and their evasion is exactly what they teach to their children.

In my effort to teach the joy of the labor of sanitizing the tableware, I regret to report abject failure. I joyfully joined in helping with washing dishes, as well as pots and pans, only to find none of my joy to be contagious. Instead of joining Daddy's joy, my children thought he must be crazy, and they gladly tried to yield to him all the dishwashing joy available. Some twenty years later, I learned the true results of my sincere efforts. After dinner at our older daughter's home, I arose as usual and took my plate and silverware to the kitchen sink. When I tried to rinse my utensils, I was sternly ordered away from the sink. I received an ultimatum: "In this house, there is a firm rule against washing dishes after dinner. In this house, we relax after a meal and give it time to digest. The dishes will be washed in the dishwasher tomorrow." End of ultimatum. As you can see, I still reflect on the lesson of the joy of labor that I taught me, even if nobody else learned it.

If I had it to do all over again, I think I might have convened a family summit, as we often did. If, then, they still planned to eat from clean dishes, they would have to vote for three teams of two each to be responsible for a week at a time. In addition, you would have to get up early enough in the morning to do the job before school, if you had not done it already. And, as I said about work in general, it is better when you learn to enjoy it. I have proved that is possible, even with dishwashing.

In fact, total inactivity is the worst curse you can endure, whether it is a recession or an oversupply of money. You can eat only so much food and wear only one pair of shoes at a time. Paul is advising a truly abundant life, no matter how much he sounds like he is being a bit strict. Tender love and tight discipline are what all of us need, as far as work is concerned. There is a lot of talk about it in the raising of Chinese children today. Whatever continent you live on, it is best, as

Paul said, to work and be responsible. The only people who enjoy doing absolutely nothing after they are rested up are either ill in body or mind or fully convinced that they have no place or value in God's creation.

Moreover, if you heard of heaven as a place of eternal rest, skip it. The word "rest" is on the stone, and that which is resting in inactivity is under the stone. Meanwhile, the most important part is eternally busy. I have not been there to see it all, but I understand that singing God's praises is the closest thing in our experience to what they do over there. Well, if that is the case (and I'm dead sure it is), then let me warn you. It takes a lot of energy to sing. You may not have much of a voice now, but you will over there, and you will enjoy using it forever. You will never be short of breath or in bad voice, and everybody's part will fit in with everybody else's.

I learned this during the Christmas season in 1941, following Pearl Harbor. I was just out of three weeks in intensive care, when a band of medics of all kinds came through the hall singing Christmas hymns and carols on the twenty-second floor of Columbia Presbyterian Hospital. It sounded so pitiful and scarce of harmony that I had to try to help them. To my surprise, when I turned on my baritone, it wasn't there. It takes lots of breath to sing bass, and I did not have a bit to spare. Not being able to sing some praise was more than I could stand. I had spent three weeks in intensive care and not shed a tear. Yet, when I couldn't pour forth some of the bottom line of those joyous carols, I broke down and cried like a baby.

It has since occurred to me that if the joy of singing here meant that much to me, weak as I was, I wondered what it must be like to sing with the angels. I was listening to our church's excellent choir, singing Dottie Rambo's "We Shall Behold Him," when I got a glimpse of the answer. The powerful, soulful soprano soloist happened to be blind. Suddenly, I broke out in tears once again. This time it was joy, and I couldn't hold it in. Like several others in the audience, I was quietly singing my part, and it was with a choir including one who here on earth sang without sight. To her, it made no difference here either. She had enough breath for that solo, and then some. Most women would not have been that strong, and I rejoiced with her in her magnificent fulfillment.

I rejoice also that Paul's reaction would have been similar. In verse 4, he told the Thessalonians that he gloried in their patience, faith, and strength to bear tribulations and persecution. He would have gloried in the way our soloist bore the tribulation of blindness and became such a marvelous blessing to us all. We all have trials, and it is wonderful that we can stay busy with our hands, minds, and voices as we glory in each other's triumphs even as we sing glory to God!

Hallelujah!

14

Youth Sunday II

THIS SERMON IS intended to stir up the gifts of our teens and young adults, but it cannot avoid being enlightening to as many as three generations. This study of Bible meanings is also a family case study, serving as the sermon's vehicle of experiential encounter—the venue where sermon hearers meet and identify with a character and share that person's experience. In this study, Timothy's family includes three generations: Tim, the main character, his mother, and his grandmother. To know Tim, you have to understand all three. In order to understand them, you have to do a bit of what I call biblical detective work. It can be fascinating for a hearer to identify with any one of the three, who becomes the hearer's ideal—heroine or hero—the one the hearer wants to be like. It is this desire that the Holy Spirit uses to move people to desire to grow.

These biblical characters come alive when we have found enough details to give what resembles an eyewitness account. Suspense will grow as hearers join in the search for common, meaningful facts. Each one is another hook to help the hearer climb aboard the story experience. The account conveys the primary behavioral purpose, which is to move admirers of Tim, a late teenager, to stir up their talents, or gifts, as he did.

One hardly needs to mention the desperate deficit in self-esteem among youth of all types of backgrounds, especially in our crowded urban ghettoes. The word is out that they are all hard to teach. However, they are easy to get to if you keep it interesting with real-life details they find familiar, easy to recognize, and relevant. To that end, four of our young people seated on the front row will join me as detectives during our biblical exploration. Each teen has a set of questions to help us find our way.

Before we start our investigation, there is one phrase, "passing for," that requires definition outside the ghetto. One example: Jews passing for Gentiles is the attempt of Jewish people to escape from one ethnic identity and pass for another. It is a real issue in this story. In reality, identity and image are at issue everywhere, especially with young people of ethnic minorities. Therefore, it is to the young people that this sermon is directed.

The moves of consciousness are built around typical questions from four youth. The celebration reports the fun and fulfillment of stirred-up gifts engaged in selfless service.

Move 1:   What are the age, abilities, and expected responsibilities of what you call youth?

Move 2:   What was behind Paul's unique compliment of Tim's mother and grandmother? (Ethno-religious faithfulness despite increased persecution)

Move 3:   What was the abundant evidence that Tim was smart, intelligent, and gifted?

Move 4:   What is the reward for all of this selfless service?

SERMON TEXT: 2 TIMOTHY 1:6-7
Wherefore I put thee in remembrance that thou stir up the gift of God, which is in thee. . . . For God hath not given us the spirit of fear; but of power, and of love, and of a sound mind.

Stir Up the Gifts

On this Youth Sunday, we look at a letter from the great and famous apostle Paul to a young dude named Timotheus. I bet they called him Tim, and that's what we'll do. Let us open up our pew Bibles and turn to 2 Timothy 1. Join me in reading together verses 5 through 7 [reading in unison]: "When I call to remembrance the unfeigned faith that is in thee, which dwelt first in thy grandmother Lois, and thy mother Eunice; and I am persuaded that in thee also. Wherefore I put thee in remembrance that thou stir up the gift of God, which is in thee by the putting on of my hands. For God hath not given us the spirit of fear; but of power, and of love, and of a sound mind."

Now leave your Bibles open, so we can do some of what you might call detective-type investigation. The young folks on the front row will raise prepared questions that you, too, might be asking. As you think about an answer, I will lead us in digging through the evidence. I will give a nod when it is time for each of you to stand with your particular query.

YOUTH 1:
Brother Pastor, you said this dude Tim was young. What does that mean in hard numbers?

PASTOR:
Glad you asked. The truth is that nobody knows exactly. Judging from various letters and circumstances, I'm guessing nineteen, or anything up to, say, twenty-one. I would have to think it could be no younger than maybe eighteen years.

YOUTH 1:
Thank you. That helps.

YOUTH 2:
Reverend, what does this word "unfeigned" mean? My pocket translation uses the word "sincere" in that spot. I could see

it as "unfaked," but my real question is why Paul is making such a big issue about it. Like most Christians aren't so sincere, already.

PASTOR:
You're a good detective. It does seem that this is just what Paul is thinking. He does not praise anybody else like that in all his many mentions of specific names.

YOUTH 2:
Well then, what did they do that was so special?

PASTOR:
That's an excellent question! I'll try to keep it short, but maybe you had better take your seat.

You see, Lois and Eunice had migrated from their hometown in Canaan (probably not Jerusalem). Like many other oppressed Jews, they had settled in Asia Minor (Turkey today), in a town of the Greek-speaking Roman Empire. Since they did not intend to return home, they started passing for Greeks. They dropped their birth names and took the Greek names we know. Eunice married a Greek, and when the baby came, they named him Timotheus. In Greek, it means one who honors God. They also chose not to circumcise him, because Eunice and Lois had flat-out left the Jewish religion and the hard treatment often given those born into the Hebrew faith. We would call them an ethnic minority.

It seems when Tim was very young, they converted to Christianity after hearing Paul preach. Paul was amazed at their sincerity. After all, converting to Christianity meant enduring even more persecution than they had as Jews. However, they took it gladly, because they were so deep into Jesus. Tim was such a follower of Jesus that he accepted ordination at a young age, upon reading this letter from Paul.

Let me put it this way. Lois and Eunice had a tremendous impact on Tim's life. Tim grew up speaking Aramaic with

Grandmother Lois and Greek with his dad. His mother, Eunice, spoke both languages. His relationship with his grandmother was very special. He enjoyed listening to her stories and learning about the old country. He spent more time with her as his mother stayed busy, as well as his father, whose culture was different. Their faith and conversion to Christianity became the foundation for his own faith and beliefs.

Do you see any similarities among families today? Does it help you understand why Paul praised them so highly?

YOUTH 2:

It sure does. I kind of feel like I know Tim already.

YOUTH 3:

I have a question: How do we know that he was so smart—so gifted?

PASTOR:

Do you think, perhaps, that Paul just might be kind and give him a pat on the shoulder to make him feel good?

YOUTH 3:

Not really. I'm just curious to know how you draw so much out of that short passage.

PASTOR:

Well, Paul is well-educated and frankly outspoken. When he says Tim has gifts, Tim has gifts. However, there is much more to it than that. They needed Tim partly because he spoke Greek and could read and write, like Paul. Keep in mind that ten of the first apostles did not read or write. Paul needed a Greek-speaking and reading successor to teach the Gentiles converting to Christ. For Tim to know the cultures and have fluency in at least two languages was a major gift. After all, you cannot go throughout the world and teach with ten single-culture illiterates and a former professional IRS man.

Paul was so sure Tim was full of smarts that he took him along when he went on some of his mission trips. The Bible has reports of Tim traveling with Paul and Silas to places like Corinth and Thessalonica, and then Paul sends Tim back by himself to represent Paul in difficult situations. That says a lot about Tim's capability, especially when you know about the tensions in the First Church of Corinth. Paul told them to treat Tim with kindness and respect (1 Corinthians 16:11). In so many words, he was telling them a young person could have wisdom beyond what you may think. In addition, he told Tim to be a good example for mature folks to follow (1 Timothy 4:12) and to let no man despise his youth.

YOUTH 4:
It sounds to me that you are saying language and culture are not the same. If so, which is more important?

PASTOR:
You are right, but language is a part of culture. You cannot get along well without both.

YOUTH 4:
Does color have anything to do with it?

PASTOR:
Yes and no. In distant, impersonal contact, color can make all the difference in relating. In closer relationships, however, cultural difference largely determines social relationships. Why don't you take your seat while I tell you about my experience with the gifts of culture and language. I tell you all this because you and I have the same gifts and the same problems that Tim and Paul had. Only most people don't know it, but we can learn. I did.

I grew up in Ohio, speaking Midwestern, middle-class, television English. The people I served as pastor came from Texas and Louisiana. They spoke with a Southern accent. To them, I sounded white. We sounded different, but we used the same dictionary. When I had been there several years, I enrolled in some language seminars and worked on a thesis on the genius of black preaching. I must have listened to two hundred sermons while doing research. Natives of Texas, Louisiana, and Arkansas preached all those good sermons. These preachers spoke educated English, grammatically and powerfully. I listened carefully with admiration. Before I finished listening, I had changed, unconsciously, to sound like one of them.

The congregation noticed the difference. The Western-born college kids were critical, because they saw it as a step backward. The forty-plus folk from down home said, "We used to say, 'We can hardly understand him now. What'll we do when he gets another degree?' But you fooled us. You're really letting the Holy Ghost use you now."

I was delighted along with them, but they were saying far more than they intended for me to hear. Here's what I believe was going through their minds:

1. You were not really in the Spirit when you used to try so hard and sounded so white.
2. We did not call you to be our pastor because we thought you were a great preacher.
3. We just knew you and liked you.
4. You helped us design and finance our new building.
5. And the older folks liked you because you were old Dr. H. H. Mitchell's grandson.

Can you imagine them not feeling the Holy Spirit's presence until I sounded like them? It was important to speak their English and *sound* like you were one of them. It didn't matter what I looked like, as long as I was willing to sound like them and become more like them. It took me twenty years to gain the gift Tim had without trying. He grew up with it. His mother was Jewish and his father Greek. He only had to choose one or the other tongue and culture. It was like shifting gears according to the condition of the hill. The very young church of Jesus Christ greatly needed those kinds of multipurpose gifts for communication. That is why Paul wanted to ordain Tim, even though many thought him too young.

I do not need to tell you that you have the same kinds of gift. That is exactly the issue I wish to raise. Teenagers today live in several worlds at the same time. You live in the culture of the majority, and you know how to speak and act in order to get the grades for medical school or that dream of a job. You may also speak a second or third kind of English and possess the style and movements necessary for acceptance by brothers or sisters on the block.

The question is, What are you going to do with your gifts? How will you manage being all things to two different worlds—being different people in different places as needed? It may be difficult, but not impossible. So do not give up. Stir it up.

It is good to know that you have these gifts, but the important thing is how you will use them. For Timothy, the use was his call to the ministry. That is why Paul urged him to accept his laying on of hands, or ordination. I suspect that Tim was not as surprised as you might be, or as I was. In addition to recognizing Tim's gift or call to ministry, Paul also sought to lay hands on him because they were very dear friends (2 Timothy 1:3-4). Because Paul was probably Tim's hero, it was not hard for him to say yes to the call of God. And we know he did, because Paul's letters often mention him being on the road with the missionary teams.

The same sort of call could come to one of us here. Most of us, however, will receive the call to live a dedicated life in some other vocation. Teachers, auto mechanics, nurses, and accountants responded to God's call to make a living helping other people. To use Paul's term, I call to remembrance my eighth-grade math and twelfth-grade physics teachers. To have such a major influence on me, they must have answered God's call to ministry as a teacher of God's children.

Miss Judd was a tiny woman, soon to retire. One day she asked me to stay after school. I was scared to death, until she slid into the seat beside me and explained that she wanted to help me with my math. She spread out my paper with the red marks and asked me a couple of questions. She answered my questions, too, and suddenly it was as if somebody had turned on the light. I could see the solution to problems with ease, and it was like that all the rest of my way through school. It was the same with Mr. Bailey in physics.

Today, more than seventy-five years later, I still call them to remembrance with great gratitude and a lump in my throat. There were other good teachers, as well. It takes only one, however, to save a struggling child's hope and rescue her or his gifts. Every trade or task, to which we answer the call, can give us similar fulfillment.

Paul had great respect for working with your hands—for skilled crafts. He himself was a skilled tentmaker. God calls all of us to do some kind of work five or six days a week, and even on Sundays, if there is need. Jobs are far more than just a way to earn money; they are callings or vocations for the long term. For a teenager, a job at McDonald's is a calling to help you build the necessary work habits and maturity for your calling later in life.

I'd like to close with one more account of a fulfilled calling. It happened in 1947, on a wintry cold and rainy Sunday afternoon, on a highway in East Texas. We were driving from the San Francisco area to New York City for a wedding. In those days, African Americans drove through the South with fear and trembling. On long trips, we tried to have relatively new and dependable wheels, as we say. We serviced our cars in the bigger cities along the way, as the welcome was likely to be warmer and the service performed by both expert and willing people of our ethnic group.

Suddenly the car stopped, and smoke poured out from under the dashboard. We were terrified. The attendant at the gas
station in the nearby village referred us to the town mechanic.
He, without hesitation, left his Sunday dinner, picked me up
at the gas station, and went straight to our car. He seemed not
to notice that we were black. In five minutes, he had taped
the short, accepted our five dollars, and bid us farewell. We,
of course, were extremely grateful customers. In fact, it was
so pleasant and expert that it seemed almost unreal. After all,
we were in the South!

Well, our elation lasted less than five minutes. When we
started the car, the windshield wipers caused another short,
and we had to call the mechanic back. He left his dinner once
again and came to our rescue without the slightest complaint.
When I tried to pay him for the additional repair, he politely
declined, saying, "I should have anchored those wires the first
time. By the way, this should have happened long ago. You
were fortunate that you didn't have any rain in California."
When I renewed my efforts to pay him, he advised me, "Stop
and help the next guy you see in trouble. I'm glad the Lord
let me help you." He waved us on, and we had not one more
speck of trouble all the way to New York City. Although the
mechanic seemed embarrassed by our thanks, we couldn't
stop thanking God the rest of the way.

In all these years, I'm still thanking God. I just pray that
all of you will find what God is calling you to do, and that
you will leave a trail of joyous souls thanking God for the
meal you cooked, the house you painted, the advice you gave,
or the way you blessed people in your daily work. I pray
that you will also be willing and unafraid to let people know
and feel Who it was who made you do it. As Paul said to
Tim about his calling: "For God has not given us the spirit
of fear; but of power, and of love, and of maturity and self-
discipline" (2 Timothy 1:7, author's translation).